Computer Control
and Security

Computer Control and Security

A Guide for Managers and Systems Analysts

William E. Perry, CIA, CPA, CISA

A Wiley-Interscience Publication
John Wiley & Sons
New York Brisbane Chichester Toronto

This publication is designed to provide accurate and
authoritative information in regard to the subject
matter covered. It is sold with the understanding that
the publisher is not engaged in rendering legal, accounting,
or other professional service. If legal advice or other
expert assistance is required, the services of a competent
professional person should be sought. *From a Declaration
of Principles jointly adopted by a Committee of the
American Bar Association and a Committee of Publishers.*

Library of Congress Cataloging in Publication Data:

Perry, William E.
Computer control and security.

  "A Wiley-Interscience publication."
  Includes index.
  1. Electronic data processing departments—
Security measures. 2. Computers—Access control.
I. Title.

HF5548.2.P4728   658.4'78   80-39936
ISBN 0-471-05235-3

Printed in the United States of America

10 9 8 7 6 5 4 3 2 1

2216740

There is a right time for everything:
  A time to study;
  A time to grow;
  A time to install new technology;
  And a time to control.
The time is right to mesh technology with control.

Preface

Recently, I had a problem with gophers and ordered an animal trap from the Catch'um Company. Each day, I eagerly awaited the mailman in anticipation that the animal trap would arrive. Finally, the big day came.

With a wave of excitement, I ripped open the box to observe the world's greatest animal trap. There for my eyes to behold was a display of bright, shiny, well-manufactured, and finished parts. It had the look of high quality.

However, to my dismay, a search through the box failed to uncover the assembly directions. How disappointing, I thought. I had all the pieces, but didn't know how to put them together.

The answer to my dilemma was simple. A telephone call to the vendor would provide me with the answer to my problem. Unfortunately, when I called the Catch'um Company, I was told the product was manufactured for "professional" animal trappers who do not need specific directions for putting the trap together. "Well then," I said, "what kind of animals is the trap designed to catch?" The representative responded that the trap was a general-purpose trap designed to catch anything from a mouse to a bull elephant. This story is familiar to systems designers and data processing managers.

Systems designers face this dilemma every day as they try to develop adequately controlled computer systems. Vendors provide capabilities, but few directions for how to use them. Users tell designers to provide solutions, but fail to specify the problem in enough detail. When controls fail, the systems analyst is blamed.

This book is intended to provide the data processing manager with strategies for controlling information systems. It will also help the systems analyst design adequately controlled computer systems based on these strategies. The approach begins by stating the risks that are unique to or increased in a computerized business environment. Knowing this, the analyst can design controls to prevent those risks from turning into a loss.

Properly designed and maintained controls are essential in today's computerized business environment. The integration of the computer into day-to-day business operations places greater importance on the accuracy and completeness of computer operations. With fewer hard copy documents, and less human intervention and surveillance, the adequacy of automated controls is the factor that ensures the integrity of processing.

WILLIAM E. PERRY

Orlando, Florida
February 1981

Acknowledgments

Controls and control violations have been with us since the beginning of human history. God proclaimed the first controls, and Adam and Eve were the first control violators. Things have not improved since then.

Over the years, I have heard all the reasons why controls are not necessary. I now know that adequately controlled systems take longer to build, restrict computer programmers from being creative, delay meeting scheduled dates, cause projects to exceed budgets, and inhibit computer people from showing initiative. However, at the same time, I have noticed that well-controlled computer systems have substantially reduced maintenance and increased user satisfaction. From this I conclude that controls are not all bad.

As an inspiration for writing this book, I am indebted to both Moses and the Congress of the United States. Moses gave us the Ten Commandments, which still remain the best set of controls in existence. Most of life's problems are caused by violating these controls. The Congress of the United States, in passing the Foreign Corrupt Practices Act of 1977, incorporated the word "control" into the vocabulary of corporate executives. Adequacy of control has been elevated from a trite phrase to the law of the land.

The concept of building controls into information strategy grew out of discussions with Wayne Gould. His help was essential and appreciated in the development of this book. A special thanks goes to Martha Platt for her help and patience in typing and structuring much of the material. As always, I am indebted to my wife Cindy, who both encourages and helps me complete projects of this kind. She has added the word control to her vocabulary and, like many corporate executives, wishes the word would go away.

W. E. P.

Contents

Computer Control
and Security

CHAPTER 1

Risks in a Computerized Business Environment

Computerized business systems are built to satisfy the information processing needs of an organization. If these systems functioned perfectly, there would be no need for controls. Unfortunately, problems occur continuously, which necessitates the use of controls to reduce the impact of these problems.

The computerization of business systems began in the late 1950s. The computer professional promised to revolutionize business systems. Systems analysts and programmers of the early 1960s believed it was only a matter of time until they became the rulers of industry.

While the data processing professionals were mastering technology, the accountants were attempting to control computers. As the cost of computers as a percentage of revenue increased, so did the controls placed on the computer by noncomputer people. This process still continues.

The computer professionals have been so intent on mastering technology that they have often overlooked control as perceived by management. Although it appeared obvious to computer professionals in the early 1960s that they would rapidly move into executive

1

management positions, this generally has not happened. The accountants who ignored technology but concentrated on controls have ascended to the corporate presidencies.

The need for control is as old as human history. Control is not a new subject, and the objectives of control remain constant. What changes are the forces requiring control and the method of control.

A two-year, $1 million study funded by the International Business Machines (IBM) Corporation concluded that "there is a need for improved controls because inadequate attention has been given to the importance of internal controls in the data processing environment."[1]

Controls traditionally lag behind technology. Bonnie and Clyde's success in bank robbery was due to their using technology for criminal purposes before law enforcement agencies used that technology. Bonnie and Clyde successfully used the automobile for robbery at a time when law enforcement officials were riding horses. However, although preventing crime is a purpose of control, it is but one of many objectives.

This book is designed to provide management, data processing professionals, and other users of computerized business applications with:

- An explanation of the problems in a computerized business environment.
- Recommendations for controls to reduce those problems.
- The criteria to use in developing data processing control strategy.
- An overview of the objectives of control.
- Approaches for designing controls.
- Methods for evaluating whether controls are effective.

MANAGING COMPUTER RISKS

Management cannot provide direction and oversight to control in a computerized environment until it understands the risks in that environment. The computerized environment not only introduces new risks but also increases many of the risks already present in a manual environment. For example, the computerized environment

[1] *Executive Report, Systems Auditability and Control Study,* The Institute of Internal Auditors, Altamonte Springs, Fla. 1977, p. 6.

poses the new risk of making the identical errors thousands of times in a very short period; it also increases the risk of security of data being violated because electronic data processing (EDP) concentrates data in one area. Once management understands these risks, it can approach computer risk as it approaches any other business risk.

Managing computer risks means not only identifying the risk but also determining its severity. Some risks require extensive controls, whereas other risks are relatively insignificant and may require no control at all. The difficulty with control in a computer environment is that in many organizations the risks have been neither identified nor described.

Some risks, such as security and computer crime, have been highlighted before. The extensive press coverage of these risks frequently magnifies their potential impact, causing too many controls to be implemented. On the other hand, the risks that result in the more significant losses, such as repetition of error and cascading of error, have received only minor attention in the press. Without understanding the magnitude of these risks, an organization cannot approach control from a businesslike perspective. What often happens is that resources are expended to control a risk not worth controlling, while major risks receive little or no control.

Compounding the problems of identifiying and describing risks is the monitoring of risk situations. Few data processing organizations have reports that identify and consolidate data processing losses. Losses resulting from crime, fire, and natural diaster are usually well known, but the more common losses, such as those associated with repetition of error, are rarely reported or consolidated.

The approach to controls presented in this book begins with identifying and quantifying risk. Until management understands the magnitude of the problem, control design is a "hit or miss" proposition. In the approach to control design, the control areas of environment, application, and operation are discussed to illustrate the most appropriate place to put controls. Although examples of control are provided, the emphasis here is on risk identification and the proper placement of controls. Most organizations know how to build controls once risks have been identified and the point at which to reduce that risk has been determined.

The book concludes with a section explaining how to evaluate and monitor the effectiveness of controls. Without this monitoring process, controls quickly become outdated and thus lose their effectiveness.

HOW CONTROLS REDUCE RISKS

A risk is the probability that an event will occur that will result in a loss (i.e., a problem). For example, if someone has a hole in the pocket where he keeps money, the chance that he may lose money from the pocket is the risk associated with that hole. He can control that risk by sewing up the hole, thus substantially lessening the probability of losing those funds. Thus the hole represents the risk, and sewing represents the control used to reduce that risk.

Risks in computerized business applications are "holes" in which information and/or assets can be lost. Controls are those measures that close those holes to an acceptable level. We need to recognize that in business it may be neither practical nor economical to attempt to reduce every risk situation to zero. For example, when we key information to computer media, such as a disk or tape, there is a risk of that data being wrong. If the entered information is wrong, there is a risk of loss due to erroneous information, such as paying employees for more hours than they work. We can lessen the risk of wrong data by key verifying the data. In other words, we enter the data twice and compare the two records, and if the two are equal we accept the data as correct. This assumes that it is unlikely for the same data entry error to be made twice, but we know from experience that this can happen. If we key verify data twice, that is, enter it three times, our likelihood of an error is further reduced. However, as we reduce the incidence of error, we increase the cost of entering data. At some point, we are forced to make a tradeoff between the probability of loss and the cost of preventing that loss.

The objective of control is to reduce the risk of loss. Organizations are vulnerable to loss from a variety of risks. Some of these risks in a computerized environment include:

- *Inadequate Systems Testing* Systems placed into production do not perform as specified. For example, the cause may be that in an effort to meet a scheduled startup date for a new computer system, the project team only conducts limited systems testing. The project goes into production on the scheduled date but produces numerous errors. Both user personnel and data processing personnel may need to devote many hundreds of hours to making corrections and adjustments. The organization may lose thousands of dollars of computer and people time and in addition may cause customer dissatisfaction because of the failure to either implement or enforce systems testing controls.

- *Out of Balance Condition*   The detail does not equal the control total. For example, the detailed customer balances in a computerized accounts receivable application are regularly reconciled to the file control total. At the same time, the controller maintains a manual balance of accounts receivable using the invoiced amount from the customer billing system and the incoming cash receipts. The two are reconciled only periodically, and when differences are uncovered it is often too costly to trace the cause of the discrepancy. There is a potential loss to the organization when application data is not regularly reconciled to appropriate control totals.

- *Loss of Data Security*   Data is stolen or compromised. Let's look at a savings and loan association that has an on-line system for its tellers. The system accounts for transactions by tellers, each of whom is identified by a secret password. However, the passwords are physically attached to each terminal, with each teller having the password "teller 1" for the first teller hired, "teller 2" for the second teller, and so on. Anyone having access to a terminal has ready access to any data within the system. The bank is subject to misuse of funds because a proper security environment has not been established.

A effective approach to designing controls to lessen loss is to establish an acceptable level of loss. For example, we could establish two keystroke errors per 1000 keystrokes as acceptable. When this is done, we can design the verification procedures to reach that acceptable level of loss. An acceptable level of loss is another way of describing an acceptable level of performance. For example, setting 998 accurate keystrokes per 1000 sets a desired level of performance.

Knowing the acceptable level of loss, we can design controls to reduce risks to that level. This concept recognizes that perfection is normally impractical and uneconomical. To tell people that they may not make a mistake is not a practical approach to control.

Some of the other tradeoffs that need to be considered when designing control are:

- *Performance versus Accuracy*   The faster people work, the greater the probability that errors will occur.

- *Cost versus Accuracy* The cost of controls should not exceed the benefits derived from those controls.
- *Flexibility (or Responsiveness) versus Control* Some controls stifle people's initiative to take action when necessary.

Designing controls in a computerized business environment should be based on the organization's information strategy. Control cannot be designed in a vacuum. It should be designed to be supportive of the organization's information strategy.

KNOW THINE ENEMY

Controls should be built *only* to reduce risk; therefore, until the risk is known, control development is ineffective. This golden rule of control should not be violated. Risks need to be identified, analyzed, and controlled, and in that order.

It is not always easy to identify and analyze risk. However, when this step is not performed, computerized applications contain many time bombs, called risks, waiting to explode. We can't control the unknown. Much of the blame laid on computers is caused by ineffective control—these tiny time bombs continually explode into errors, omissions and losses.

Controls should be designed using a process similar to that used for systems development. In fact, many people refer to "systems" of control, which implies an orderly process of development. A methodology for designing controls is illustrated in Figure 1.1 and explained as follows:

- *Identify the Risks* Know what you are trying to control.
- *Determine an Acceptable Loss due to Risk* Risk normally cannot be reduced to zero economically; therefore, management must state what level of loss it can live with.
- *Develop a Control Strategy* Plan the organization's control strategy hand in hand with the other data processing strategies.
- *Develop Control Development Procedures* Create the needed policies, procedures, and methods to implement the control strategy.
- *Build a Strong Control Environment* Management must support control by establishing an environment that encourages people to believe that control is important.

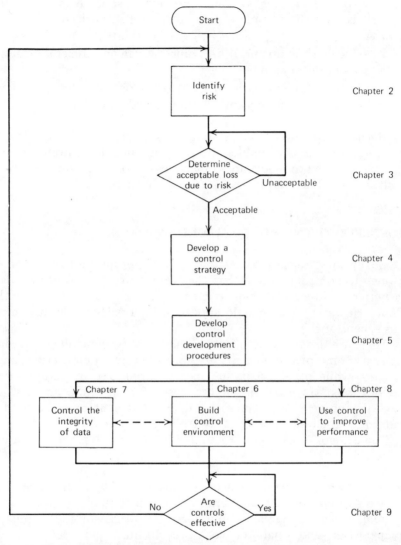

Figure 1.1 **Methodology for Designing Controls.**

- *Control the Integrity of Data* Provide reasonable assurance that data is accurate, complete, consistent, and authorized.
- *Use Control to Improve Performance* Control aids management in achieving the organization's objectives in an efficient, effective, and economical manner.
- *Assess the Effectiveness of Controls* Controls remain effective only when they are continually monitored and adjusted.

Management must first determine its risks or vulnerabilities and then agree on an acceptable level of risk. Once this is done, controls can be designed to meet those objectives of control. However, the installed controls should be cost-effective for these risks.

COST-EFFECTIVENESS OF CONTROLS

Good business sense dictates that it is inappropriate to spend more money to control an event than the event is worth. In other words, it is better to lose $100 then to spend $200 to avoid the loss of that $100. However, what would appear to be a golden rule of controls has exceptions.

There are several types of events that must be controlled regardless of cost. Some of these events are controlled by computerized applications, while other events are merely monitored by computerized applications. However, when the cost of controlling an event far exceeds the economic benefit, prudent judgment must be used to determine the best method of controlling that event.

The categories of events that must be controlled regardless of cost include:

- *Violations of Law* Organizations must provide the necessary controls to ensure that they are in compliance with the law. For example, if the Wage and Hour Law states that employees must be paid time and a half for work over 40 hours per week, then controls must be put into place to ensure compliance with that law.
- *Organizational Ethics* Organizations are judged as stewards of their resources. Some alleged types of misuse of resources warrant extensive controls. For example, the misuse of small amounts of resources by corporate officers for which personal gain is suspected is viewed much more harshly than normal business risk. Therefore, many organizations install uneconomical controls to

provide assurance that senior management's personal expenses comply with organizational policy and intent.

- *Sensitive Transactions* Certain events are more sensitive or visible than other events. For example, the control and movement of radioactive material, or dumping of chemicals, require much more extensive control than the movement of normal commercial inventory or the disposal of normal waste.
- *Public Safety* Organizations cannot afford frequent adverse publicity caused by potentially harmful products. Some safety measures are legislated, but others are just good business practice. Many times, controls must be able to trace the raw materials in defective products back to their production batch or source.

When an organization assesses the need for installing controls, it must consider both the events being controlled and the cost-effectiveness of controlling those events. Some events must be controlled regardless of cost. However, in most instances a cost-effectiveness evaluation should be made to determine the economics of controlling the event.

Defining Controllable Events

Most organizations have many thousands of individual controls. This is particularly true in computerized applications. Examples of individual controls in computerized applications include check digits, data field edits, comparison of a key field to a master file to validate authenticity, batch totals, and so forth. In many instances, it would cost more to conduct the cost-effectiveness evaluation than it would to design, install, and operate these individual controls.

The cost-effectiveness evaluation should be made at the risk level. To the casual observer, there are an infinite number of controls, but a finite number of risks. Thus risk becomes not only the determinant for designing controls, but also the basis for the cost-effectiveness valuation.

Let's examine two risks in a computerized order entry/billing application. The risks in this application are that (1) orders will not be received by the system, and (2) the product will be shipped but not billed. In most order entry/billing systems, there are only about 15 to 20 risks to be considered. On the other hand, there may be several thousand controls installed to reduce those risks to an acceptable level. If we examine the risk of purchase orders not being received, we find that the losses associated with that risk are intangible. The loss is of customers who will not reorder. The question that we must then ask is, if an order is lost, how many customers will not attempt to replace that order? This is the measure of true loss. If we decide that risk is minimal, then controls may not be necessary. However, the risk of shipping a product and not billing it is a very real risk with an immediate loss. Therefore, it is much more likely that we would want to control that risk than the one dealing with lost orders.

A question of equal difficulty is the performance of the cost-effectiveness calculation. Prerequisites to that calculation are the determination of the potential loss due to that risk and the determination of an acceptable level of loss. For example, if risk X would produce a $1000 loss without control, and management says that only a $100 loss is acceptable, then controls must be installed that reduce the risk from $1000 to $100. This establishes the upper limit on what controls can cost (i.e., $1000 minus $100, or $900 for the maximum cost of controls).

Benefit of Controls

In the example just discussed, the benefit is reducing the loss from $1000 to $100, or a $900 benefit. Although the calculation sounds easy, in practice it may not be. For example, the risk might be lost customer orders due to the inability to fill an order within a 24-hour period or the risk of embezzlement of funds from the cash drawer in a retail establishment. Difficult as they may be, however, it is these difficult-to-make decisions that are needed to quantify the benefits received from reducing a risk. Without this type of information, control placement is strictly judgment and intuition.

Cost of Controls

There are two general categories of cost associated with controls: development and operation costs. The sum of the two provides the cost of implementing a control.

The cost of controls should be the cost of all the controls used to reduce a specific risk, but it normally is not practical to accumulate the cost for each control, especially the small controls. Therefore, some rules of thumb need to be established for costing individual controls. For example, an organization may decide that it costs an average of $100 to design and implement an on-line computer control, such as an edit, and $50 a year to operate that control. Using these rules of thumb significantly simplifies the accumulation of cost.

The key controls normally will be individually costed. Both development and operation costs involve people time, computer costs, overhead costs, and special out-of-pocket items, such as the purchase of disks, forms, and so on. These are basically the same costs used in any other data processing cost calculation.

Are Controls Cost-Effective?

Once the costs and benefits have been determined, the actual calculation is a mechanical function. However, it is not as straightforward as adding all the benefits and subtracting from the total all the costs to determine whether the control is cost-effective. Two other factors must be included in the calculation. These are the value of money and the effective life of the control. For example, benefits received a year from now are not worth the same value as money expended to design controls today. In addition, the benefits must be extended over the useful life of the controls, whereas the development cost is incurred only once.

CHAPTER 2

Identifying Risks

There are two approaches to designing controls. One is designing controls to accomplish a specific control objective, such as ensuring accurate data. This is a positive approach to control design. The second approach is to determine what prevents control objectives from being achieved and then to design controls that lessen those risks. This is a negative approach, but normally the more effective one.

Many systems analysts design controls using the positive approach. For example, when they want to be assured that data is accurate, they will design controls to help achieve this objective. They will build controls that key verify data, develop batch totals, and add check digits to selected fields. The problem with this approach is that the analysts may not anticipate what can go wrong.

Designing controls using the negative, or risk, approach concentrates the control efforts on the weak links. For example, when designing controls for the control objective of data is accurate, the first step is to determine why data will not be accurate or, in other words, the risks preventing accurate data. One of the reasons that data might be inaccurate is the risk that it would be misrepresented. For example, if a product is boxed in groups of

100, a customer might indicate that he or she wants 100, meaning one box. If the quantity ordered is listed as 100 boxes, rather than 100 units in one box, the quantity is misrepresented. When this risk is recognized, controls can be built to lessen the risk. For example, any order over 99 might put out an error message for verification that the order is stated in cartons and not individual units.

This chapter explains the unique or increased problems in a computerized business environment.

CAUSES OF RISK

Risk is the probability that an event will occur that will cause a loss. If these causes can be identified, the risk can be reduced. Thus not only do we need to identify the *risk*, but we also must identify the *cause* that can turn that risk into a loss.

One of the risks we continually face is that of heart disease. This risk is affected by many causes, among them smoking cigarettes. Thus the risk of heart disease is increased for someone who smokes cigarettes. A control to reduce this risk is low-tar cigarettes.

We need to identify all the causes of the risk if we hope to reduce the risk to an acceptable level, because many of the causes increasing risk are additive. For example, in the risk of heart disease the sum of the following causes is greater than each one individually:

• Smoking cigarettes.
• Being overweight.
• Having high blood pressure.

One of the difficulties with risk in a computerized environment is that a loss is often associated with a sequence or chain of conditions or events. Changing the probability of one link in the chain will affect the total probability. Consider the following chain of events relating to a security risk:

• *Cause 1* An individual can gain access to the terminal—probability, 60%.
• *Cause 2* An individual without a password could acquire a password—probability, 10 percent.
• *Cause 3* An individual could gain knowledge about how to use a system—probability, 40%.

- *Cause 4* The chance that an individual would be motivated to browse, given the opportunity—probability, 30%.

If this chain of events occurs, it could cause the loss of privacy. Now, what can a systems designer, user, or manager do to control the risk? Note that in this scenario the issue is a security problem (unauthorized activity). This typically receives only minimal attention by the systems designer using risk probability. However, an analyst could restrict access for any given password to only a portion of that data, hence reducing the loss potential.

THE RESULTS OF RISK (PROBLEMS)

The question of interest to the EDP professional is, "What will be the result of the new and increased risks in a computerized business environment?" These results of EDP risks are the problems caused by the new or increased losses. The results help the systems analyst, programmer, manager, operator, or user understand why time and effort should be expended to control these risks.

The EDP problems presented in this book have been categorized to facilitate designing controls. The problems that are unique to or increase in a computerized business environment are:

- *Improper Use of Technology* Losses associated with the failure to use technology properly.
- *Cascading of Errors* Losses associated with a multiplying effect of one error causing another error, which causes another error, and so on.
- *Illogical Processing* Losses associated with unusual processing that most people would detect as an error, such as a payroll check for $1 million, if people were processing the data.
- *Inability to Translate Needs into Technical Requirements* Losses associated with the inability of technical people to communicate the capabilities of the computer with users having a need for but not an understanding of the computer, and vice versa.
- *Inability to Control Technology* Losses associated with the use of the technology exceeding the ability of people to control the data processed using that technology.
- *Repetition of Errors* Losses associated with programs following the same erroneous logic on every transaction of that type.

- *Incorrect Entry of Data* Losses associated with translating data to machine-readable media.
- *Incorrect Use and Interpretation of Data* Losses associated with users of computer data making bad business decisions due to misunderstandings of the accuracy, completeness, consistency, or timeliness of data.
- *Concentration of Data* Losses associated with placing large quantities of data in a centralized data base.

The risks that are magnified in a computerized business environment are:

- *Inability to React Quickly* Losses associated with the difficulties in extracting data or changing processing to reflect new needs.
- *Inability to Substantiate Processing* Losses associated with either the cost or complexity of obtaining evidence to support computer processing.
- *Concentration of Responsibilities* Losses associated with concentrating responsibilities in a single system or among a few people.

Each of these problems is discussed individually in this chapter, showing the most common causes of the problems.

HUMAN CONCERN ABOUT PROBLEMS

Management has the responsibility for control. This responsibility cannot be delegated, but the authority to take action can be. It is unrealistic to expect management to be aware of the types of controls that are effective in computerized applications. What management must be aware of are the problems associated with a computerized environment. Once these problems are recognized, management can provide the necessary resources, direction, and support so that the losses associated with those problems can be reduced to an acceptable level.

The functions that can address the new and increased problems are:

- *Senior Management* Officers of the organization.
- *Data Processing Management* Those individuals responsible for data processing.

- *Systems Development* The systems analyst who helps define the feasibility of a system and then develops the systems specifications so that systems solutions can be automated.
- *Programming* The conversion of design specifications into executable programs.
- *Operation* Running the system on the computer to produce the desired results.
- *User* Providing data for, relying on, and using the results of processing in the day-to-day operation of the organization.

Data processing management should be aware that it should provide some environmental control direction if applications are to be designed in a cost-effective manner. For example, data processing management should be involved in the establishment of such controls as:

- Physical access security.
- Data dictionary.
- Security software systems.
- Encryption and compaction capability and training in their design implications.
- Job accounting systems.
- Testing or simulation facilities.
- Monitoring and planning facilities.

Similarly, programmers should know what they should address in applications, for example, process logic, validation of data entry, or exception reports. And finally, senior management must understand its part in developing a consistent and controlled environment (i.e., strategy).

Each level of responsibility has certain topical areas or risks that it should address. People tend to look at risk and controls to see not that risks are controlled but that they are consistent throughout the environment. Usually, only management and probably senior management can adjust the level of control. If management opts for more control when the alternative is presented, then people at lower levels will start to logically and consistently tighten controls. If management asks about controls, employees below will do a good job of addressing them. Without management attention, controls may be erratic; good designers will do a good job, but others will merely go through the motions. After all, workers tell themselves, "people do what management checks—if something isn't checked, why worry about it?"

Management is concerned with the total operation, but subfunctions within data processing are really only concerned with the problems that affect a specific job. Therefore, as the causes of problems are discussed, they will be identified with the function in the best position to reduce losses associated with those causes.

Improper Use of Technology

One of the challenges facing data processing personnel is the proper use of technology. As computer technology becomes more complex, so does this task. It is difficult for one person to keep abreast of all aspects of computer hardware and software. Thus it often requires a team effort of "experts" in different areas to properly utilize the technology.

The reasons for improper use of technology include:

- High turnover of data processing project personnel.
- Overdesigning of the computer system.
- Use by systems and user personnel of new technology for technology's sake.
- Insufficient skills among members of the project team.
- Use of unproven hardware.
- Use of unproven software.
- Unrealistic expectations on the part of users.

The improper use of technology occurs for many of these reasons because the systems analysts and programmers do not recognize when they are in trouble. If problems are not recognized early in the design process, their impact is magnified. When the problems are uncovered, project personnel often attempt to correct and compensate for these problems, not recognizing the magnitude of the problem and its impact on the user.

The most common results of the improper use of technology are listed in Exhibit 2.1. The causes show the extent of this problem. The improper use of technology can shift work that might best be done on the computer to people, and vice versa. It also causes the uneconomical use of both computer hardware and software. These

Exhibit 2.1   Problem: Improper Use of Technology

Result of Problem	Corrective Action Responsibility
Misuse of people	Data processing management
Misuse of technology	Systems development
Uneconomical use of technology	Systems development
Inadequate service level	Operation
Data destroyed	Operation
Over budget	Data processing management
Not on schedule	Data processing management
Out of date	Data processing management

causes of problems can result in users not receiving service adequate to meet their needs.

Cascading of Errors

A unique problem in computerized business applications is the cascading of errors, which occurs when one error triggers a series of errors. This problem has plagued data processing people since the inception of the computer. It is also a difficult problem to prevent and sometimes to detect.

Often it is difficult to determine the cause of the cascading error. For example, an error in one system may result in adding a character to a position in a field or record that is normally blank. This may not cause any problem in the system where the error occurs, but may trigger problems in another system that uses that data. Suppose, for example, that one system assumed a field to be six characters in length, while another system treated it as seven characters; if the seventh character that normally is blank is suddenly changed to a nonblank, it would cause errors in the second system.

Cascading errors can be caused by the following types of conditions:

- Information added to a normally unused data position.
- Recompilation of the program without adequate testing.
- Overflow of a numeric field (e.g., putting 1000 in a three-position field).

Exhibit 2.2   Problem: Cascading of Errors

Result of Problem	Corrective Action Responsibility
Data error	Programming
Unreliable data	Programming

- One unplanned-for condition triggering more unplanned-for conditions.
- Hardware or software error.
- Change in the sequence in which data is entered.

The results of cascading of errors, showing the scope of this problem, are listed in Exhibit 2.2. They normally result in either erroneous or unreliable data.

Illogical Processing

Many of the stories making headlines about computers involve illogical processing. People enjoy reading about the mistakes machines make. Mistakes of this type that are caught are usually very large mistakes. They occur because computerized business applications prform functions exactly as instructed. Whatever the computer is instructed to do, it does. Whether the results are logical or illogical is unimportant to the computer.

In manual or partially computerized systems, people oversee transactions. When something is illogical, it is normally noticed. For example, when a large payment is applied to an account with a small balance, the clerk posting that transaction would suspect a problem and verify whether the payment belonged to that account. In a computerized application, this human surveillance may not occur. The computer would apply that payment, resulting in a large credit balance in the account.

Illogical processing usually occurs as a result of a malfunction. The types of malfunctions that can cause illogical processing are:

- A printer hardware failure (e.g., an extra character prints in a high-order position in a numerical field).
- Vendor hardware or software failure.
- A programming error.

- An input error.
- Erroneous master information, such as wrong prices for a product in a master file.

Exhibit 2.3 lists the causes of illogical processing problems. The causes are all associated with application processing. Thus they affect the completeness, accuracy, and consistency of data.

Illogical processing results in data being erroneous, misclassified, misrepresented, unreliable, and omitted. All these results cause data processing to be incorrect. Most undetected illogical processing involves only a few transactions. When illogical processing is repetitious, such as printing every payroll check for $1 million, the errors are normally caught quickly.

Exhibit 2.3   Problem: Illogical Processing

Result of Problem	Corrective Action Responsibility
Error of omissions	Programming
Misclassifications	Programming
Misrepresentations	Programming
Data error	Programming
Error of commission	Programming
Unreliable data	Programming

Inability to Translate Needs into Technical Requirements

One of the continuous problems of data processing is the correct translation of user needs into technical requirements so that the needs can be programmed for a computer. There are two major impediments to this process. The first is the inability of nondata processing people to comprehend the intricacies of a computer. The second obstacle is the fact that a computer system must be preprogrammed for all possible error conditions. Unfortunately, people normally handle problems after they occur rather than anticipating and providing for errors before they occur.

There are many approaches that help users understand computer concepts. In some organizations user personnel are sent to data processing schools prior to the inception of computer applications in their department. In other organizations data processing personnel are transferred to the user department to help them specify their requirements. Still others require users to become involved in preparing test data and acceptance testing of the system as a means of ensuring that they understand systems capabilities.

Users who do not understand computer capabilities:

- May not understand how to use computer outputs properly.
- Will not know what can and cannot be done on a computer and therefore will either fail to specify some implementable need or ask for requirements that are not economical to implement.
- Cannot distinguish input problems (i.e., manual problems) from processing problems within the computerized application.
- Are unable to specify changes that can be readily incorporated into the existing application.

One of the most difficult problems facing a user is anticipating and specifying error conditions. In a manual system, when an error occurs a member of the user department analyzes the situation, confers with a supervisor, and establishes and implements a course of action. At the time the error conditions occurs, the facts of the situation are known. In a computerized application, this same scenario must be enacted prior to the error's occurrence. Rather than knowing the facts, however, the user department must guess what the situation will be and specify a course of action based on that estimate.

If the user fails to specify error conditions, and they occur, illogical processing may result. To avoid this situation, many data processing personnel incorporate their own guesses as to what may happen and establish a course of action based on that guess. Because the data processing department's determination of future errors may not coincide with what the user would do should that situation occur, it is best for the user to make this determination.

The control objectives and vulnerabilities associated with the inability to translate needs into technical requirements are listed in Exhibit 2.4. The vulnerabilities show the magnitude of this risk. Note that the control objectives affected are those associated with application controls.

The failure to translate user needs into technical requirements affects the accuracy, completeness, consistency, and authorization of data. When the systems analyst and the user are not properly communicating, it affects the classification and representation of

Exhibit 2.4   Problem: Inability to Translate Needs into
Technical Requirements

Result of Problem	Corrective Action Responsibility
Cutoffs	User
Misclassifications	User
Misrepresentations	User
Unreliable data	User
Uncomparable data	User
Data not processed according to generally accepted accounting principles	User
Data not fairly presented	User
Invalid data	User
Violation of management policy	User
Illegal transaction	User
Unethical transaction	User
Out of date	User
Solves wrong problem	Systems development

data as well as recording data in the wrong accounting period. These misunderstandings of requirements can result in invalid data being accepted, unintentional violations of management policy, and transactions processed in an illegal or unethical manner. Any of these situations can cause data to be processed contrary to generally accepted accounting principles and thus not fairly presented. The net result is unreliable and uncomparable data.

Inability to Control Technology

The methods of controlling technology invariably lag behind the use of that technology. This is common in most professions. For example, in the medical profession diseases must be isolated before cures can be found. In the legal profession, situations must occur in society before laws are written to regulate those situations.

The fact that control lags behind technology is understandable, because the causes associated with technological problems must first be uncovered. For example, data base technology posed some concentration of data concerns that required special recovery controls. However, until the impact of data concentration was known, the necessary controls were difficult to establish.

The highly technical nature of data processing poses some unique problems. For example, the systems development process is filled with threats to developing a successful system. In the early days of data processing, the complexities of systems development were not fully appreciated. Without recognizing these problems, data processing personnel made estimates and promises that were unrealistic. This caused management in many organizations to totally disregard data processing estimates and to ask accountants to develop costing procedures for new computer applications.

On-line applications pose some new threats to data because data within the communication network is in various stages of processing. Should the system fail, it is often difficult to reconstruct which transactions have been entered but not processed, which have been partially processed, and which have not been entered. New data problems occur whenever new technology is introduced. Some of the equipment posing control problems now are cash dispensing terminals, supermarket checkout optical scanners, and point-of-sale terminals.

Closely allied with controlling technology is the ability to reconstruct processing. Most control problems can be overcome if adequate retrievable evidence is available to substantiate processing. Large on-line data base files pose difficult reconstruction problems. Among them are broken pointers within the data base, retrieval and sequencing of information on data logs, and the reconstruction of data in queues.

Exhibit 2.5 enumerates the many results of the inability to control technology. Note that technology affects all areas of control.

Performance is affected by the systems development process. This results in systems not being developed on schedule or within budget. Poor systems development may mean that the operation of the completed system will be inefficient. The ability to substantiate and reconstruct transactions affects the availability and integrity of data. The inability to process data correctly affects the accuracy and completeness of data.

Exhibit 2.5   Problem: Inability to Control Technology

Result of Problem	Corrective Action Responsibility
Over budget	Data processing management
Not on schedule	Data processing management
Error of omission	Systems development
Cutoffs	Systems development
Data error	Programmer
Temporary loss	Programmer
Inadequate audit trail	Systems development
Data destroyed	Operations
Processing facility inoperable	Operations
Unreliable data	Systems development
Uneconomical use of technology	Systems development
Improper use of technology	Operations
Out of date	User

Repetition of Errors

The computer is designed to process data consistently. However, this processing can be consistently right or consistently wrong. If the processing rules are in error, so will be the results of processing.

When people process transactions, they too make mistakes. Industry is often warned to watch out for events that occur on Monday morning or Friday afternoon, as these are times when errors tend to be made. However, if a clerk makes a mistake on an adding machine, it may occur only on a single transaction. This poses control problems, but not of the repetitious type.

The type of problems in computerized applications that cause errors to be repeated include:

• Errors in programming the computerized application.
• Hardware errors, such as a print position not functioning correctly.
• Use of the wrong form for input or output.

- Change in the computer system that has not been communicated to users.
- Changes in the user area, affecting the computer system, that have not been communicated to the computer personnel.

The results of the repetition of errors are listed in Exhibit 2.6. This problem is especially large. Repetition of errors in a data-oriented error. The results of repetitious errors affect the accuracy, completeness, and authorization of data. These result in data errors, errors of omission or commission, and invalid data being accepted into the computer system.

Exhibit 2.6   Problem Repetition of Errors

Result of Problem	Corrective Action Responsibility
Error of omission	Programming
Data error	Programming
Error of commission	Programming
Invalid data	Programming

Incorrect Entry of Data

Data processing requires that data be translated to machine-readable form. In many applications this translation is necessary so that data can be processed by a computer. For example, data recorded on a paper form may need to be keyed to computer media through a device such as a keypunch or key-to-disk device.

This entry of data into a computer adds a new possibility for error. Data may be correctly recorded by people, but altered incorrectly when entered into the computer system. For example, a keypunch operator might transpose numbers. There are many reasons why data is entered incorrectly.

Errors can occur in the entry of data into computerized applications for the following reasons:

- Source data is illegible.
- Source data does not conform to systems specifications.

- Data is entered in the wrong field or fields. For example, the number 10 is recorded so that it implies 100, or the quantity ordered is entered into the price field.
- Data is entered with a keystroke error.
- Incorrect translation of words to computer codes, such as translating a state name to a wrong state code.
- Data is not entered and an erroneous default option is selected; for example, if a clerk fails to enter the quantity ordered, the computer system may automatically select an order quantity of one, which could be erroneous.

Exhibit 2.7 lists the results of the incorrect entry of data. Note that the causes all occur during the application processing of inputted data.

The incorrect entry of data can result in numerous error conditions. Among these are data errors, errors of omission, and errors of commission. Data can also be misclassified or misrepresented. Any of these error conditions can affect the recording of the data in the proper accounting period. In addition, data entry errors can cause unauthorized transactions to be entered and processed by the computerized application.

Exhibit 2.7   Problem: Incorrect Entry of Data

Results of Problem	Corrective Action Responsibility
Error of omission	User
Misclassifications	User
Cutoffs	User
Data error	Programmer
Error of commission	User
Misrepresentations	User
Invalid data	Programmer

Incorrect Use and Interpretation of Data

People using data without some appreciation of the application systems processing may make erroneous decisions due to a misinterpretation of that data. These people view the data from the wrong perspective. The problem is increased in a data base environment when diverse users begin to use common data.

Some of the reasons for the incorrect use and interpretation of data include the following:

- A complete report is not received.
- Data is not complete.
- User does not know the period covered by the data.
- User is unaware of special report preparation processing.
- Data is erroneous.

Many of these reasons occur with secondary or casual data users, who make invalid assumptions and then rely on those assumptions. Much of this incorrect use can be avoided by placing a narrative description of the data in the report on the first page of the report.

The results of incorrect use and misinterpretation of data problems are listed in Exhibit 2.8, which illustrates the problem's magnitude. The erroneous decision can result in a direct loss of revenue, by erroneously denying a customer credit, for example, or in an indirect loss caused by ineffective operations.

Concentration of Data

The use of computer media, such as tapes and disks, centralizes data. Data base technology not only centralizes data but makes it readily accessible. This provides two opportunities to better meet the needs of users. At the same time, however, data base introduces new and increased risks.

The centralization of data makes it possible for multiple users to share data as a resource of the organization. The multiple use of the same data eliminates many data redundancies and helps ensure data consistency.

The concentration of data brings together data elements that were previously separate. For example, in a nondata base environment, payroll data may exist in one system, personnel data on employees in another system, job data that is employee related in another system, and so on. In a centralized data base, all data associated with one employee may be centrally stored and accessible. This poses new threats to data security that did not exist when data was scattered among different systems.

Exhibit 2.8   Problem: Incorrect Use and Interpretation of Data

Results of Problem	Corrective Action Responsibility
Untimely delivery	Operations
Modified data	Systems development
Manipulated data	Systems development
Invalid data	Systems development
Misuse of technology	Systems development
Data error	Programming
Unreliable data	Programming
Error of omission	Programming
Misclassifications	Programming
Misrepresentations	Programming
Error of commission	Programming
Uncomparable data	User
Data not processed according to generally accepted accounting principles	User
Data not fairly presented	User
Cutoffs	User

Data base information is managed by a single software system called a data base management system (DBMS). The use of these DBMS's enables data to be maintained independently of the applications that use that data. Using a DBMS enables access in the data base to any or all data, which is retrievable in any format. Without proper controls, data is subject to modification and manipulation.

The introduction of independently maintained data bases requires changes in organizational structure because a new function must be established to administer the data. In many organizations, this is called the data base administration function. The function may exist within the data processing department, or a high-level data administrator might be appointed to oversee the use of data within the organization.

The results of the concentration of data are listed in Exhibit 2.9.

Exhibit 2.9   Problem: Concentration of Data

Result of Problem	Corrective Action Responsibility
Lack of detection	Data processing management
Compromised data	Data processing management
Loss of privacy	Data processing management
Accessibility	Data processing management
Modified data	User
Manipulated data	User

The results show how large this problem is. The primary control to lessen this concentration of data risk is limiting access to data to authorized people with authorized purposes for accessing that data. Without those controls, data may be manipulated or modified without detection. This results in a loss of data integrity. However, equally important are the compromise of data and the loss of privacy to individuals. In these instances, data is taken, but still resides in the data base. This is a serious threat to many organizations whose data is confidential or to whom the loss of data could result in a loss to the organization. For example, in the aerospace industry in a time of shortage of skilled engineers, compromising the payroll information may result in the pirating of many key engineering personnel. If the compromise of payroll information is not detected, the company may never know how outside groups were able to make the "right offer" to their employees.

Inability to React Quickly

Computerized business applications are composed of many thousands of individual instructions. These instructions process large files incorporating perhaps millions of individual pieces of data. The result is a highly structured system designed to accomplish some specific tasks. Using these systems for other than their intended purposes may be difficult.

As new needs arise, people must react to those new demands. Frequently, they need information from the computerized application instantaneously. The foresight of the system's designers determines whether that need can be quickly satisfied.

The types of events that occur requiring a quick reaction include:

- A telephone call or visit requesting some specific information, such as an account balance.
- A program stoppage that needs to be fixed immediately.
- A required system change, such as a new tax requirement or a change by a federal regulatory agency, or when a new product or price needs to be added to a master file.
- Evidence to support questionable processing.
- Information for management and/or auditors.

One of the stated advantages to data base systems is their ability to react more quickly to the needs of users. This is generally true; however, it is still dependent on the flexibility designed into systems by analysts. Some of the newer extract languages, such as query and report writing languages, help facilitate the extraction of data. This is especially true in on-line systems.

The results of the risk of an inability to react quickly are listed in Exhibit 2.10. The inability to react can occur because the system is out of date with user needs. In those instances the system may not have the information necessary to satisfy a user need. Systems also cannot react quickly when the system's design has not solved the appropriate user need or when an adequate audit trail has not been developed. In other instances the needed data is in the system but the system cannot provide the needed data quickly. This can occur because the data cannot be immediately located or the time to react, such as overnight processing, is not in harmony with the needs of the user.

Exhibit 2.10   Problem: Inability to React Quickly

Result of Problem	Corrective Action Responsibility
Out of date	User
Solves wrong problem	Systems development
Untimely delivery	Operations
Temporary loss	Operations
Inadequate audit trail	Systems development

Inability to Substantiate Processing

One of the challenges facing systems designers is maintaining evidence sufficient to substantiate the processing that has occurred. This may involve verifying the processing of a single transaction, such as an individual employee payroll record, or the totality of processing, such as supporting the gross payroll amount for a specific pay period. The types of evidence needed vary from application to application.

Processing must be substantiated from individual transactions to account balances and from account balances to the supporting individual transactions. For example, if the gross pay amount for a pay period is to be substantiated, the system must be able to provide all the individual pay records that were used to produce that amount. Another type of substantiation that is necessary is proving that an individual transaction is included in the account balance. However, the more common substantiation of processing deals with individual transactions.

In substantiating an individual transaction, three types of support are needed. First, the input data must be properly transcribed to the computer record. Second, other information used in processing the transaction (e.g., master data) must be properly selected. Third, the processing of the data must be performed properly.

The substantiation may involve the following types of information:

- Source documents.
- Master information.
- Before and after images of updated information.
- Administrative policies and procedures stating processing rules.
- Evidence that the data was properly transmitted to other systems.
- Evidence that the data was properly accumulated in all appropriate accounts.

Several problems and difficulties occur in substantiating computer processing, including the following:

- Loss of intermediate records.
- Split audit trails making the coordination of the two parts difficult (e.g., one part maintained by the application and one part maintained by the DBMS).

- Processing segments of a transaction over an extended period of time, so that the audit trail is split among numerous days (e.g., processing part of an order today, another part next week, payment in 6 weeks, product return in 10 weeks, etc.).
- Referencing by other than a primary reference (e.g., finding a specific social security number in a file ordered by employee number).

Exhibit 2.11 shows the results of the inability to substantiate processing. The two threats are loss of integrity of data and the inability to recover from a problem. If data is modified or manipulated, either intentionally or unintentionally, the integrity of data is lost. The integrity from a substantiation viewpoint is lost if the audit trail is inadequate or missing. The loss of data, the processing facility, or key people may make substantiation impossible. Controls should assure that these vulnerabilities do not turn into losses.

Exhibit 2.11   Problem: Inability to Substantiate Processing

Result of Problem	Corrective Action Responsibility
Modified data	Systems development
Manipulated data	Systems development
Inadequate audit trail	Systems development
Data destroyed	Operations
Processing facility inoperable	Operations
Key people lost	Data processing management

Concentration of Responsibilities

One of the strongest principles of control in a manual system is the concept of segregation of duties. (This concept states that no one individual will have complete control over the transaction. For example, the individual who deposits funds into a bank should not have the authority to withdraw funds, and vice versa. By splitting the duties, one individual checks the integrity of another.)
In computerized applications, this concept still applies but must

be implemented differently. In other words, the ability to control a complete transaction may reside within a single computer system.

This concentration of responsibilities in the computer without adequate controls poses a risk of manipulation and modification of data. It also poses the possibility of unauthorized data being accepted into the computerized applications.

The segregation of duties concept appears to be adequately satisfied in batch-oriented systems. This is because batched systems often have built-in redundancy of data, with different departments controlling different data parts of a transaction. For example, the billing department can control the debits to accounts receivable in a batch accounts receivable system, while the treasurer may control the cash or credits to accounts receivable with an independent cash receipts system.

When organizations move to on-line data base technology, the concentration of responsibilities risk appears in a new form. In an on-line data base application, data is maintained independently of the computerized applications. In addition, the data base may be under the control of a single individual called the data base administrator. This necessitates new methods of control to segregate the new responsibilities.

The results of the concentration of responsibilities are listed in Exhibit 2.12. The results show the magnitude of this problem. These

Exhibit 2.12   Problem: Concentration of Responsibilities

Result of Problem	Corrective Action Responsibility
Modified data	Data processing management
Manipulated data	Data processing management
Invalid data	Data processing management
Violation of management policy	Senior management
Illegal transaction	Senior management
Unethical transaction	Senior management
Lack of detection	Senior management
Compromised data	Data processing management
Loss of privacy	Data processing management
Accessibility	Data processing management

vulnerabilities affect the integrity and authorization of data. Without proper controls, data can be modified or manipulated, or the authorization rules established by management can be avoided.

AFTER RISK IDENTIFICATION, WHAT HAPPENS?

Once the risk and its potential results have been identified, a determination must be made whether the organization can live with the risk. This obviously requires an estimate of the severity of the risk. If the organization can live with the risk, no further action need be taken. On the other hand, if the risk is greater than the organization desires, controls should be implemented to reduce the risk to an acceptable level.

CHAPTER 3

Living with Risks

The successful management of risk in the data processing environment is the key to efficient business practice. Risk is ever present and requires management attention. Risk management can best be performed when the manager has assessed the following information.

- The new and increased problems in the data processing environment (covered in Chapter 2).
- The causes of those problems (covered in Chapter 2).
- The differences in the data processing environment that lead to the causes of risks.
- The data processing function that is in the best position to reduce those causes.
- The acceptable level of loss resulting from the problems.

WHAT'S DIFFERENT ABOUT A COMPUTERIZED ENVIRONMENT?

When comparing a computerized business environment to a noncomputerized one, there are some significant differences. The following difference categories are selected to emphasize activities subject to control:

- Human functions replaced with machines.

- Coded data not readable by people.
- Rapid processing.
- Errors preprogrammed.
- Automation of control.
- Centralization of functions.
- New forms of evidence.
- New methods of authorization.
- New processing concepts.

These differences between a computerized business environment and a noncomputerized one help us understand where to place controls. Some of these are obvious; for example, the concentrations of functions in a computerized business environment require new methods of control to ensure that an adequate segregation of duties exists. However, the fact that a computerized business environment creates new forms of evidence does not always result in controls that ensure the appropriate recovery, availability, and audit trail necessary to substantiate and support processing.

Let's look at these differences individually.

Human Functions Replaced with Machines

An obvious difference between a computerized environment and a noncomputerized one is the fact that the computer performs functions that were previously performed by people (see Figure 3.1). Some of these functions are relatively simple, such as accumulating financial totals, whereas others, maintaining adequate levels of inventory, for example, are much more complex. The controls required vary according to the complexity of the task and the quantity of the automated tasks.

This conversion from manual to computerized tasks requires developing all the detailed instructions needed to perform the human tasks on the computer. The difficulty in this is that the computer performs very low-level tasks, such as adding and subtracting, whereas people perform higher-level tasks, such as determining inventory replenishment quantities. The problem is further complicated because many tasks performed by people are performed using human judgment. Judgment is difficult to program, and only algorithms representing the judgment process can be programmed. Thus the systems analyst is faced with the challenge of converting judg-

Figure 3.1   Human Functions Replaced with Machines.

ments into algorithms. Many of these algorithms are extremely complex, but fortunately when these algorithms are continually improved the judgment is frequently performed better by the computer than by people.

Coded Data Not Readable by People

Another difference between computerized and noncomputerized systems is the method of storing information (see Figure 3.2). In noncomputer systems the storage method is almost always paper. Assuming that the paper can be located, the information is readily understood by people.

In a computerized application information is stored in a machine-readable format. This normally means information is stored using a representation of codes that can be read by a machine using a code structure based on a yes or no condition. This is further complicated by the fact that a large amount of computer data is coded. In other words, because of the characteristics of the computer, it is easier to code information. For example, a one-position code can represent gender, so that if that position is coded M, it means male, and if

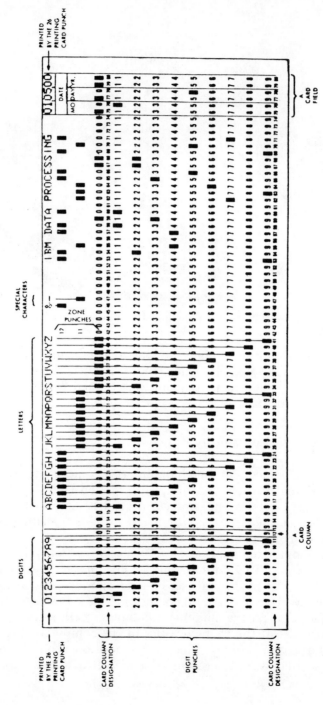

Figure 3.2 Coded Data Not Readable by People.

38

coded F, it means female. Not only is the information difficult or impossible to read when on the computer media, but even after being translated, it may not be in an interpretable state.

There are other complications in storing machine-readable information that cause interpretation problems. These complications include the following:

- Data is stored contiguously; in other words, no spaces exist between different elements of data.
- Positions of data change over a period of time. Thus information that was in the third and fourth positions of a record a year ago may now be in the seventh and eighth positions.
- Unused characters in a record may contain meaningless information.
- Some computerized information, such as packed decimal, cannot be printed as a single character.
- Information may be compacted for storage or transmission, which eliminates unwanted information; it takes an algorithm, however, to convert the data back to its original state.

Rapid Processing

Computers perform tasks faster than people (see Figure 3.3). It is possible for a computer to do certain jobs a million or more times faster than a person. In fact, this is what the computer is all about. The speed and accuracy of a computer enable it to perform the millions of detailed instructions necessary to accomplish a task in a reasonable period of time.

This speed is changing the way many organizations operate. In a noncomputerized environment, or even in a batched-oriented environment, there was normally "think time" available during processing. For example, a customer would give an order, and the company could manually check the credit, the availability of inventory, and so on. People were accustomed to waiting while these processes occurred.

In an on-line data base computerized business environment, people are demanding instantaneous action. For example, computer systems can provide an instant verification of a customer's credit. This has obvious processing advantages, but it also has control disadvantages. There is no margin for error or second thoughts in an instantaneous decision. If credit is extended for a purchase, it is extended. There is

Figure 3.3 Rapid Processing.

no walking over to a supervisor or making a phone call if the computer gives the go-ahead. Thus the time previously built in for human supervision, additional checking, and the like, is no longer present.

Electronic funds transfer and other computerized networks will accelerate the speed at which transactions are processed. This increased speed necessitates increased attention to control. Errors in programming, bad business logic, or changing conditions can quickly result in large losses.

Errors Preprogrammed

Good computer practice dictates that what can go wrong should be preprogrammed into the computerized applications (see Figure 3.4). Ideally, the computer logic solves the error condition. However, where is it not practical to work out the solution in advance, the processing can be temporarily suspended awaiting human intervention.

There are four general methods of correcting errors recognized by a computerized system. These are:

- *Automatic Correction* The systems will "guess" what the correct value is. For example, if a code can be M or F, and an N is en-

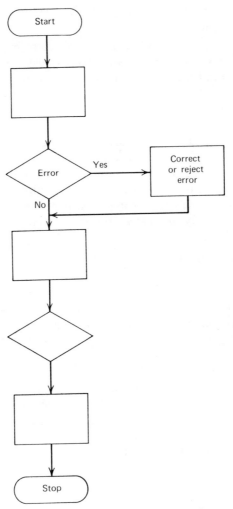

Figure 3.4 **Errors Preprogrammed.**

tered, the computer could guess that an M was meant and that a keystroke operator had misread the handwriting and entered an N.

- *Default Option*   The computer system substitutes the most logical value for an unrecognizable or unentered value. For example, if a method of shipping is not specified, the computer system can indicate ship-by-parcel-post. This concept can save people the time of entering data when the normal condition occurs very frequently.

- *Reject the Data*   The computer system requests human intervention to make the correction.
- *Warning*   The system requests human oversight to verify the correctness of the data when an error is suspected. For example, if data indicated that an employee worked more than 99 hours a week, it would be logical to verify that this actually occurred and was not a data entry error.

Many users and data processing personnel find preprogramming error conditions difficult. However, using the risk scenario outlined in this book, systems analysts can do a much better job of preprogramming error conditions. Risk analysis requires the analyst to continually ask "What can go wrong?" rather than only programming the rules that properly process correctly entered data.

Automation of Control

Control is automated in many computerized business applications, and more and more of the manual control functions in computerized applications are being automated (see Figure 3.5.) For example, in the data base environment, access controls over data are being automated using security profiles.

The more controls that are automated, the less human oversight remains over computer processing. This continues to shift the reliance on machines to automatic control processing in lieu of using people. This means more reliance on the accuracy and completeness of automated controls.

Examples of controls that used to be manual that are being automated include:

- Transaction authorization, such as the entry of a password to authorize a withdrawal from a cash dispensing terminal.
- Automatic initiation of a transaction, such as the replenishment of inventory when it falls below the reorder quantity.
- Approval of customer credit.
- Electronic transfer of funds.
- Computer-generated dunning notices.
- Reconcilation of account balances to details, such as that accomplished by programming in lieu of a redundant external control.

Figure 3.5 Automation of Control.

As with other aspects of computerized applications, the automation of control requires detailed specifications. Because the execution of many controls in a manual environment exercised judgment, that judgment must be automated. It should be recognized that the automation of control ensures consistency of control; however, that consistency can be either right or wrong.

Centralization of Functions

Computer systems have the capability of bringing many functions together in one central location (see Figure 3.6). There are three types of centralization: (1) the centralization of systems, (2) the centralization of data, and (3) the centralization of the data processing systems and programming function.

The centralization of systems is necessary in most organizations. There is a natural flow of data between systems, and a centralization of systems facilitates this flow. Even when systems are "distributed," there is still an inner connection and a central tying together of systems.

Figure 3.6 **Centralization of Functions.**

There is a strong technological movement toward the centralization of data. It has been estimated that during the 1980s most organizations will utilize the data base concept. With centralization of data goes centralization of the administration of data. Centralization of data is advantageous because it eliminates data redundancy and increases data consistency.

Most organizations have centralized their data processing functions. Because data processing is becoming more complex, there is a need for experts in different areas. For example, there are operating systems experts, computer language experts, DBMS experts, and communication experts. We can expect this tendency to increase as technology advances. Because few organizations can afford many of these experts, it is logical to assume a continual centralization of the data processing function.

Communication lines enable the decentralization of hardware and processing capabilities. However. This should not be confused with the centralization of functions. What communication lines provide is increased reliance on the data, systems, and computer experts at the central location.

New Forms of Evidence

In 1971 the Internal Revenue Service officially recognized computer records as official records of the organization (see Figure 3.7). This fact had been recognized by most major corporations years earlier. Even before 1971, however, corporations were sending government agencies reels of tape containing payroll tax information.

Traditional legal evidence for business applications includes:

- Preprinted forms.
- Signatures.
- Initials.
- Time and date stamps.
- Seals.
- Organizational logos.

The input and output of data on computer terminals frequently eliminate these types of evidence. In their place are such things as:

- Passwords.
- Entry of magnetically encoded cards.

- Operator identification codes.
- Access to a terminal location.
- Verification of the existence of internal codes, such as a customer number.

As the evidence changes, so does the media on which it is stored. Some of the new media include:

- Computer tapes.
- Magnetic disks.
- Diskettes.
- Microfilms.

Many of these new forms of evidence have yet to be tested in the courts. For example, it is generally accepted that entering a magnetic card and a password in a cash dispensing terminal is sufficient evidence that an authorized depositor withdrew funds. However, this concept has yet to be adequately tested in the courts. Although there is no reason to believe that it would not be accepted as valid evidence, it represents but one of many changes in how transactions are substantiated that awaits judicial verification.

Figure 3.7 **New Forms of Evidence.**

New Methods of Authorization

Authorization is one part of evidence that an authorized transaction has occurred (see Figure 3.8). The evidence of transaction processing should indicate how that transaction was authorized for processing.

Figure 3.8 New Methods of Authorization.

The new methods for authorizing terminal-entered transactions include:

- Passwords.
- Magnetically encoded cards.
- Passwords plus a magnetically encoded card.
- Entry of a supervisor key into a terminal.

Computer vendors are experimenting with many new types of authorization methods. The most promising at the current time appears to be verification of a signature made on a cathode tube using a light pen. However, other methods being explored include fingerprints and voiceprints.

New Processing Concepts

Much of the computer revolution is due to the automation of business applications (see Figure 3.9). This automation enables the system to be used more efficiently and economically. It also increased the accuracy of processing and the availability of reports in different formats.

The systems proving most valuable are those incorporating new processing concepts. These are concepts that were neither economical nor possible with manual systems. Examples of some of these newer concepts include:

- Point-of-sale equipment for recording sales, checking credit, updating inventory, and so on.
- Cash dispensing terminals.
- Instantaneous analysis of data by means of processing languages, such as query.
- Consistency of data throughout the organization by eliminating data redundancy.
- Instant status of the organization's activities, such as the airline reservation systems.

The new processing concepts are changing the way organizations do business. It has been predicted that the changes in the next 10 years will exceed those in the preceding 20 years. Thus not only will many office functions be automated, but the methods by which they are automated will change the way offices function as well.

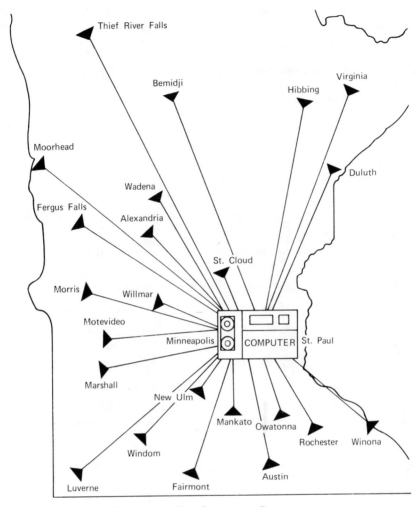

Figure 3.9 **New Processing Concepts.**

ASSIGNING RESPONSIBILITY FOR IMPLEMENTATION OF CONTROL

Senior management has the primary responsibility for control. This involves the establishment of a strong control environment (see Chapter 6). Most of the implementation of controls can be assigned. It is important that the best suited function be assigned the responsibility for implementing the control.

Controls are implemented to reduce the problems, and, therefore, the responsibility to implement controls should be designated according to the potential result of the problems. Exhibit 3.1 shows the recommended assignments for control responsibilities.

Exhibit 3.1   Recommended Control Responsibility Assignments

Organizational Function	Result of Problem	Problem
Senior Management	Violation of management intent	Concentration of responsibilities
	Illegal transaction	Concentration of responsibilities
	Unethical transaction	Concentration of responsilibies
	Lack of detection	Concentration of responsibilities
Data Processing	Misuse of people	Improper use of technology
	Over budget	Improper use of technology
		Inability to control technology
	Not on schedule	Improper use of technology
		Inability to control technology
	Out of date	Improper use of technology
	Lack of detection	Concentration of data
	Compromised data	Concentration of data
		Concentration of responsibilities
	Loss of privacy	Concentration of data
		Concentration of responsibilities
	Accessibility	Concentration of data
		Concentration of responsibilities
	Key people lost	Inability to substantiate people

Exhibit 3.1 (*Continued*)

Organizational Function	Result of Problem	Problem
	Modified data	Concentration of responsibilities
	Manipulated data	Concentration of responsibilities
	Invalid data	Concentration of responsibilities
Systems development	Misuse of technology	Improper use of technology
		Incorrect use and interpretation of data
	Uneconomical use of technology	Improper use of technology
	Solves wrong problem	Inability to translate needs into technical requirements
		Inability to react quickly
	Error of omission	Inability to control technology
	Cutoffs	Inability to control technology
	Inadequate audit trail	Inability to control technology
		Inability to react quickly
		Inability to substantiate people
	Unreliable data	Inability to control technology
	Uneconomical use of technology	Inability to control technology
	Modified data	Incorrect use and interpretation of data
	Manipulated data	Inability to substantiate people

Exhibit 3.1 *(Continued)*

Organizational Function	Result of Problem	Problem
	Invalid data	Incorrect use and interpretation of data
Programming	Data error	Cascading of errors
		Illogical processing
		Inability to control technology
		Repetition of error
		Incorrect entry of data
		Incorrect use and interpretation of data
	Unreliable data	Cascading of errors
		Illogical processing
		Incorrect use and interpretation of data
	Error of omission	Illogical processing
		Repetition of error
		Incorrect use and interpretation of data
	Misclassifications	Illogical processing
		Incorrect use and interpretation of data
	Misrepresentations	Illogical processing
		Incorrect use and interpretation of data
	Error of commission	Illogical processing
		Repetition of error
		Incorrect use and interpretation of data
	Temporary loss	Inability to control technology

Exhibit 3.1 (*Continued*)

Organizational Function	Result of Problem	Problem
	Invalid data	Repetition of error
		Incorrect entry of data
Operations	Inadequate service level	Improper use of technology
	Data destroyed	Improper use of technology
		Inability to control technology
		Inability to substantiate people
	Processing facility inoperable	Inability to control technology
		Inability to substantiate people
	Improper use of technology	Inability to control technology
	Untimely delivery	Incorrect use and interpretation of data
	Temporary loss	Inability to react quickly
User	Cutoffs	Inability to translate needs into technical requirements
		Incorrect entry of data
		Incorrect use and interpretation of data
	Misclassifications	Inability to translate needs into technical requirements
		Incorrect entry of data
	Modified data	Concentration of data
	Misrepresentations	Inability to translate needs into technical requirements
		Incorrect entry of data
	Manipulated data	Concentration of data

Exhibit 3.1 *(Continued)*

Organizational Function	Result of Problem	Problem
	Unreliable data	Inability to translate needs into technical requirements
	Uncomparable data	Inability to translate needs into technical requirements
		Incorrect use and interpretation of data
	Data not processed according to generally accepted accounting principles	Inability to translate needs into technical requirements
		Incorrect use and interpretation of data
	Data not fairly presented	Inability to translate needs into technical requirements
		Incorrect use and interpretation of data
	Invalid data	Inability to translate needs into technical requirements
	Violation of management policy	Inability to translate needs into technical requirements
	Illegal data	Inability to translate needs into technical requirements
	Unethical data	Inability to translate needs into technical requirements
	Out of date	Inability to translate needs into technical requirements
		Inability to control technology
		Inability to react quickly
	Error of omission	Incorrect entry of data
	Error of commission	Incorrect entry of data

Acceptable Level of Risk Determination

Both risk and loss are unavoidable. Risks cannot be eliminated because it is an ever-present threat. For example, the risk due to the improper use of technology will always exist. The fact that technology is used involved the risk of its improper use. Loss is normally associated with something going wrong. Therefore, unless all human errors, mistakes, acts of God, and so on, can be eliminated, loss will occur.

The option available to systems analysts is to reduce the probability of that loss to an acceptable level. This is accomplished through the use of controls. However, the amount of control is dependent on the level of risk that a user of a computerized business environment is willing to accept.

Let's look at a simplified example. A key-to-disk operator enters order entry information. Assume experience has shown that the average keypunch operator will make one error per 1100 keystrokes. If the manager of the order entry department feels that one keystroke error per 1100 keystrokes is acceptable, then the acceptable level for that risk has been established. In that situation, no controls are necessary so long as the acceptable level of loss proves to be the actual loss. However, if the manager of the order entry department indicates that only one error per 2000 keystrokes is acceptable, then additional controls must be implemented to reduce the error rate from one per 1100 keystrokes to one per 2000 keystrokes. For this, the analyst has a variety of controls, such as training, key verifying, form simplification, and so forth. In actual practice, keystroke errors would have to be oriented to specific fields. Obviously, a keypunch error in an individual's first name is not nearly as serious as a keypunch error in the amount to be paid to a vendor. One causes a slight inconvenience, perhaps, while the other may result in an overpayment to a vendor and thus a direct loss of cash.

In many instances, it is more practical to quantify loss in terms of dollars because few risk situations are as clear-cut as the number of keystroke errors per thousand keystrokes. For example, losses due to fire or entering a wrong price in a computerized application and errors resulting in underpaying or overpaying employees are best measured in dollar amounts.

Risk analysis is a method of quantifying an acceptable level of loss. There are two items of information necessary to perform risk analysis. The first is the impact of the loss each time it occurs. The second part of risk analysis is determining the frequency of the loss events.

Determining an acceptable level of loss is a two-step process, as follows:

- Determine the probable loss assuming there are no controls.
- Use this probable loss estimate to make a managerial judgment as to what level of loss is acceptable.

Until management has a feel for a probable loss, it is difficult to make a judgment about an acceptable level of loss. A probable loss shows the magnitude of loss, which provides management with guidance as to the risk for that specific situation. Without this preliminary loss estimate, unrealistic acceptable levels of loss may be either tolerated or determined.

Let's look at a risk analysis example using the entry of a wrong price in a computerized billing application. If a wrong price is entered, we must estimate how much will be the impact of that wrong price. Let us assume that it will be $10. Then we must estimate the frequency with which that price will be used in our billing system. Let's assume that it would be used once per day. Thus the net loss for entering one wrong price would be approximately $2400 per year, based on one loss for each of the 240 work days. This provides us with an estimate of the probable loss. Knowing this, we can then make a managerial judgment as to an acceptable level of loss. This acceptable level of loss must be determined so that managerial judgment can be applied in deciding how much control is necessary.

The difficulty faced in determining a probable level of loss is estimating both the impact and the frequency of each loss situation. A risk analysis technique using multiples of 10 for impact and frequency has proven effective. In this process, the only impacts considered are in multiples of 10. The first step is to consider the lowest impact. For example, the lowest impact considered may be 10¢, $1, or $10. Once that has been established, however, each impact will be a multiple of 10 higher, such as $10, $100, $1000, and so on. The same logic is used for frequency when we consider whether it occurs 10 times per day, once per day, once every 10 days, once every 100 days, and so forth.

The risk analysis matrix illustrated in Figure 3.10 can be used to quickly calculate the probable loss for some of the risk situations. The left-hand side of the matrix shows eight levels of impact for a loss. These range between $10 and $100 million. Across the top of

	$i=$ $f=$	Once in 300 yrs (100,000 days) 1	Once in 30 yrs (10,000 days) 2	Once in 3 yrs (1,000 days) 3	Once in 100 days 4	Once in 10 days 5	Once per day 6	10 per day 7	100 per day 8
$10	1					$300	$3,000		$300k
$100	2				$300	$3,000	$30k	$300k	$3M
$1000	3			$300	$3,000	$30k	$300k	$3M	$30M
$10,000	4		$300	$3,000	$30k	$300k	$3M	$30M	
$100,000	5	$300	$3,000	$30k	$300k	$3M	$30M	$300M	
$1,000,000	6	$3,000	$30k	$300k	$3M	$30M	$300M		
$10,000,000	7	$30k	$300k	$3M	$30M	$300M			
$100,000,000	8	$300k	$3M	$30M	$300M				

Figure 3.10   Risk Analysis Matrix.

the matrix are eight levels of frequency, ranging from once in 300 years to 100 times per day. The intersection in the matrix shows the estimated loss for most of the impact times frequency calculation within the given ranges. For example, a $100,000 loss (impact range number 5) for a frequency of once in 300 years (frequency range number 1) is $300.

USING RISK KNOWLEDGE

It take time and effort to collect accurate information about risks. Once collected, this risk information should be put to work to reduce those risks. The process needed is the development of a control strategy by senior management. The implementation of this strategy can then be delegated to data processing management and users.

CHAPTER 4

Developing a Computer Control Strategy

The computer control strategy governs the origination, processing, storage, and use of data. The strategy may be planned and directed by management or it may just happen by default. The objective of this chapter is to identify the components of computer control strategy so that management can plan and implement an effective and efficient control strategy.

Computer control strategy establishes a climate and need for control. The strategy determines not only how information is used in an organization, but also the type of risks that occur in using that information. For example, one aspect of computer control strategy is the competency of computer employees hired. Highly competent people can build better computer applications than less competent people. Therefore, there is a higher risk of loss to the organization when hiring people with lesser skills. The information strategy determines the skill level of people hired by the organization. This strategy may be determined by salary levels, as opposed to a direct act by mangement stating their policy is to hire only people with average skills, but it is determined by management strategy. One type of control that helps lessen the risks associated with less skilled computer employees is to rely more on purchased applications.

Because strategy is such an integral part of control design, it must be understood prior to designing controls. An organization's computer control strategy establishes management's intentions and concerns about controls. This is particularly true of the means used to achieve objectives. Much of the intervention by government into controlling the internal operations of corporations is related to the organization's apparent disregard of the means used to achieve objectives (e.g., when a company bribes government officials). Controls not only help achieve objectives; they also monitor the means used to reach those objectives.

DESIGNING A SYSTEM OF INTERNAL CONTROL

There are almost as many approaches to designing controls as there are organizations. Part of this is attributable to the fact that business and information strategy vary so much among organizations. A major factor for this variance in the approach to controls is the varying attitudes among managers regarding the need for and objectives of control.

There is little doubt of management's responsibility for control in the organization, and management cannot avoid it. The Commission on Auditors Responsibilities established by the American Institute of Certified Public Accountants (AICPA) stated that "management is responsible for establishing and maintaining controls over the accounting system."[1]

The Special Advisory Committee on Internal Accounting Controls established by the AICPA stated in its tentative report dated September 15, 1978, that:

> The internal control environment established by management has a significant impact on the selection and effectiveness of a company's accounting control procedures and techniques.
>
> A poor control environment would make some accounting controls inoperative for all intents and purposes because, for example, individuals would hesitate to challenge a management override of a specific control procedure. On

[1] Report, Conclusions and Recommendations by the Commission on Auditors Responsibilities," Commission on Auditors Responsibilities, New York, 1978, p. 55.

the other hand, a strong control environment, for example, one with tight budgetary controls and an effective internal audit function, can have an important bearing on the selection of effectiveness of specific accounting control procedures and techniques.[2]

The ways management establishes a control environment in the computer area is through a computer control strategy. The AICPA's Special Advisory Committee on Internal Accounting Controls further stated that this environment is so important that other controls may not be effective if the environmental controls are weak. This is illustrated in Figure 4.1. The figure shows that application and operational controls are surrounded by the environmental controls that, in turn, are influenced by information strategy. These influences are particularly strong in the EDP area. The design of environmental

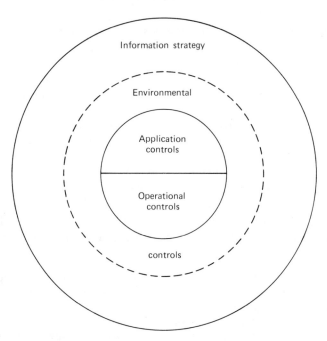

Figure 4.1   **Designing a System of Internal Control.**

[2] "Tentative Report of the Special Advisory Committee on Internal Accounting Control," American Institute of Certified Public Accountants, New York, September 15, 1978, p. 9.

controls directly affects the effectiveness of the applications and operational controls.

Computer control strategy has been divided in this book into the following areas to emphasize the impact of this strategy on control design and effectiveness:

- Diversity of data use.
- Accessibility to data.
- Sharing of business systems.
- Data independence.
- Competency of people.
- Selection of computer technology.
- Systems development process.
- Data processing controls.

We will examine each of these areas of control strategy, emphasizing the impact on controls.

Diversity of Data Use

Most data processing systems share data. Sharing in a nondata base environment means that when one application is finished using data, another application can use that data. In a data base environment the two applications can share the same data concurrently.

Most of the sharing that occurs in data processing is among homogenous users. For example, all users within the accounting area may share common data. The information about customer billing is shared with the credit department, the customer billing department, the inventory control department, and the financial analyst. Most of the people in these departments report to the same individual and have a common understanding of and need for the reliability and consistency of data. This type of sharing causes few problems.

Diverse users are defined as users having different reliability and consistency needs for data. Let's examine the needs of two diverse users in a job accounting system. The two diverse users might be the manager of the production department and the manager of the accounting department. The data in question is the number of hours reported by employees chargeable to specific jobs. The accounting manager is concerned that the hours reported are the same as the hours paid; the reliability of the hours reported for each job is not as important as the fact that the total hours reported as worked have actually been worked. On the other hand, the production manager needs accurate hours worked on a job so that the schedules and costs can be estimated for similar jobs in the future. The production manager may also use that information to evaluate the performance of people. The production manager is vitally concerned and wants controls that help ensure the time reported for a specific job represents actual time worked on that job. To the accounting manager that is not as important as other aspects of the data.

If the computer control strategy of the organization is to permit diverse users to use the same data, then the reliability and consistency of data for all parties must be considered. This involves the procedures for the collection of data, the verification and accuracy of data, the reporting of data, and the controls that ensure the data is reliable, consistent, and received on a timely basis.

An important consideration with diverse users is the timing of data, because diverse users have different needs regarding the reporting of transactions. In an example involving the recording of a sale, the diverse users might be the manager for inventory and the accounting manager. The inventory manager wants sales reported as they occur so that inventory can be set aside until those orders are filled and so that new inventory can be ordered as soon as needed. On the other hand, the accounting manager does not want to record the sale until the product is actually shipped, which may be many days or weeks after the order is taken. Therefore, the accounting manager does not want that information entered into the sales system because it would conflict with generally accepted accounting practices. This is an example of a diverse user conflict that needs to be resolved in the systems design.

Strategy is not all black or white. Rarely do all diverse users in an organization use a common data element. Equally as rare would be an organization in which there were no diverse users sharing a common data element. Therefore, most organizations can be placed somewhere on a data diversity continuum. At one end of this continuum is the organization that has no diverse users of data, and at the other end is the organization with complete diversity of data use (see Figure 4.2, which illustrates the continuum). Most organizations fall somewhere on the continuum between the two extremes.

On all the computer control strategy continua, there is a low-risk end and a high-risk end. Where the organization falls on each continuum is the first determination a control designer must make. If the organization falls near the low-risk end of the continuum, con-

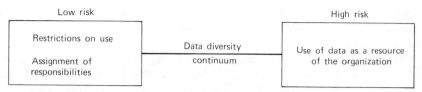

Figure 4.2 Diversity of Data Use.

trol need not be as strong as when the organization falls near the high-risk end.

The characteristics indicating that an organization is at the low-risk end of the diversity of data use continuum include:

- *Restrictions on Use* The use of data is restricted to those purposes for which it is designed. This normally requires data redundancy. For example, data designed for pay purposes is restricted to that use. If data is needed for job scheduling and planning purposes, a redundant system may be established for that purpose.
- *Assignment of Responsibilities* One individual is held responsible for the reliability, consistency, accuracy, and timeliness of an individual data element. All users of that data element must work through the responsible individual, who can act as a control point to resolve or explain data reliability.

The characteristic that places an organization on the high-risk end of the data diversity continuum is the *use of data as a resource of the organization.* This means that all diverse users have access to all data elements. When this happens, it is important that executive management, and not individual users such as the payroll department, controls the data.

The computer control strategy on diversity of data use affects systems decisions about input and maintenance of data to ensure that the data is consistent with each user's needs. Data use means much more than just the right to extract existing data or use reports that include the data. The results of this strategy affect the organizational structure established to maintain and control the data.

Accessibility to Data

Accessibility to data was one of the great social issues of the 1970s. It was during that decade that the public became concerned about information privacy and the use of data. The computer made information about individuals readily accessible, and, when that data was incorrect, many individuals were denied credit, jobs, and other items of importance to them.

When data is erroneous and made readily accessible, people's lives can be quickly and broadly affected through no fault of their own. As more of these problems were given coverage by the press, new laws were passed regarding the accessibility of information. These privacy laws, coupled with new technological advances that enabled data to be even more accessible, contributed to an awareness of the need to control that accessibility.

Organizations have a computer control strategy for the accessibility of data. Again, these strategies may be formally introduced or may result from practice. The considerations that need to be addressed in the accessibility strategy are:

- Accountability.
- Privacy.
- Confidentiality.
- Security.
- Legal implication.
- Authorization.

Management should decide who can have access to which data element(s) and for which purpose(s). The determination of accessibility rights to data should encompass the criteria just listed.

Accountability must be an integral part of accessibility strategy. People should be held accountable for data elements, and records should be maintained of who accesses those data elements so that that responsibility can be monitored. When management establishes its accessibility policy, it should design and implement the controls to enforce that strategy.

The characteristics that indicate a low risk on the data accessibility continuum include (see Figure 4.3):

- *Privacy Policy* A corporate policy exists regarding the handling of employee information. Obviously this policy must adhere to federal and state laws, but may extend beyond legal requirements. It should cover the people who can see personal information about employees or customers, as well as what those employees or customers can see of the information maintained by the organization about them.

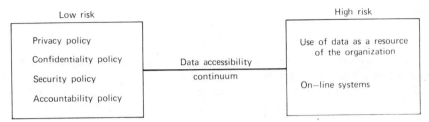

Figure 4.3 **Accessibility of Data.**

- *Confidentiality Policy* The military has a strict policy for classifying the confidentiality of data. Many private industries also classify their information according to a confidentiality policy. This includes procedures for marking documents, the special storage and movement of confidential documents, the accountability of use, and the destruction of the documents.
- *Security Policy* A security policy deals with the physical and logical protection of data. For example, the policy might allow only computer operation personnel in the computer center, restrict use of security profiles, and enforce automatic terminal shutdown after a specified number of invalid access attempts.
- *Accountability Policy* This policy covers the method and procedures of making people accountable for their acts, which can include assigning responsibility for data elements, keeping logs of usage, and so forth.

The criteria that indicate an organization is at the high-risk end of the accessibility continuum include:

- *Use of Data as a Resource of the Organization* When data is readily available to all users in the organization, it increases the accessibility to the data elements within an individual's area of authorization, and it also increases accessibility to all data within the data base.
- *On-Line Systems* When data can be accessed over communication lines, it is more readily accessible than when obtained from a system without communication facilities.

The computer control strategy for accessibility of data defines to whom and for what purpose the data is available. The strategy should also include the controls that are necessary to enforce the organization's accessibility policy and procedures.

Sharing of Business Systems

The computer control strategy of an organization should include the use and ownership of systems. The systems plan should be consistent with the plan for organizational structure. For example, if the organization is highly decentralized, then most likely the systems will be decentralized. On the other hand, if the organization is highly centralized, we could expect a centralization of information systems.

Some organizations have a multiplicity of redundant systems. Each operating division, for example, may design and implement its own payroll application. This gives payroll autonomy to operating divisions. Other organizations use common systems to perform common functions, such as payroll, for the entire organization.

One of the stronger control techniques is redundancy. This involves collecting the same data and/or performing the same task two or more times and then verifying the results. Redundancy is used by management in many organizations as a control. For example, if the personnel department maintains a complete record of employees, and the payroll department maintains a complete record of employees, a crosscheck between the two systems verifies the accuracy or inaccuracy of the systems.

When management uses redundancy as a control, there is a limited sharing of systems. The redundancy inherent in multiple systems helps provide management assurance of the accuracy and completeness of the data.

As systems are shared, redundancy is decreased. This means more controls are needed in common systems to provide the same degree of ensurance that is possible with redundant systems. However, redundant systems normally do not provide the same data consistency that is possible in shared systems.

The criteria that are indicative of low risk in a system sharing continuum include (see Figure 4.4):

- *Decentralization* Departments or divisions have autonomy in selecting and implementing the computerized applications they want. One department or division is not obligated to share either data or processing with another group.
- *Data Redundancy* The same data is maintained independently in two or more computer systems within the organization.
- *Departmental Systems* Systems are considered "owned" by the department that uses them. This is often the result of an accounting billout system in which the development and opera-

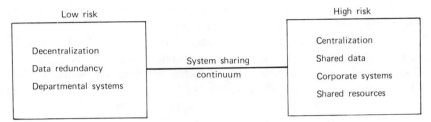

Figure 4.4 Sharing of Business Systems.

tion of a computer system is charged back to the initiating department. In these instances, department managers feel that their department bought and paid for the system and consequently that the system is theirs.

The criteria that indicate high risk in the system sharing continuum include:

- *Centralization* Processing is shared by two or more departments or divisions. A common payroll system would exemplify this kind of centralization.
- *Shared Data* Data redundancy is reduced by having multiple users use the same data element.
- *Corporate Systems* The computerized systems are considered processing systems of the corporation and thus are not "owned" by the using departments.
- *Shared Resources* The same hardware and software is used by multiple users, as opposed to each department or division operating its own computer.

The computer control strategy involved in the sharing of business systems often depends on management involvement. If management is not heavily involved in information systems, the individual applications will become the property of the using departments. It is only through the active involvement of top management that the needed coordination can be achieved.

Data Independence

Data independence means maintaining data independently of the programs that use that data. In other words, it splits data processing into its two segments, data and processing. The data is maintained by one group, and the processing by another.

Date independence is implemented through establishing a data base. A data base is a collection of individual data elements as opposed to records. Nondata base systems use records, whereas data base systems structure data elements into records at the time of execution. Thus in a data base there are no records, and the user has the option of changing the information wanted at execution time.

An important advantage of data independence is that users get only the data elements they need. In the record concept, when a program requests one element of data, it receives the entire record. This permits programs to have access to information that perhaps they should not have access to. This does not happen in a data base environment, because the data base delivers only those elements that are needed and thus protects the privacy of unwanted data elements.

The data base concept makes using data as a corporate resource practical. It is only when multiple users can access the same data element concurrently that management can consider the strategy of organization-managed data.

Very few organizations use data base in the context of an organizational resource. Most data bases are currently used as a sophisticated access method. When one application system establishes a data base for use only by that application, it uses data base as an access method. This is valuable for any program within the application, because it is not restricted by record structures. However, the impact on control of using data base in this format is minimal.

The criteria indicating that data independence is at the low-risk end of the continuum include (see Figure 4.5):

- *System-Owned Data* Each system "owns" the data that that system uses. If data is shared, it is on an after-the-fact basis, as opposed to concurrent sharing.

- *Centralized Data Documentation* Detailed documentation describes each data element, its attributes, the edits to be performed on that data element, who can access it, what purposes it can be accessed for, how much can it be changed during an access (e.g., plus or minus 10% of the current value), the retention period of the data, who is accountable, and so on. With this type of documentation, users of the data have a full understanding of the data element characterisitcs.

- *Active Data Dictionary* This software system enforces data documentation by only permitting programs to access data that has been documented according to the organization's standards.

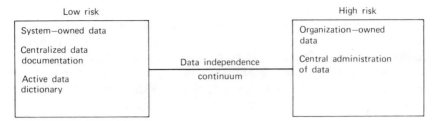

Figure 4.5 **Data Independence.**

The criteria that indicate an organization is at the high-risk end of the data independence continuum include:

- *Organization-Owned Data* The data used in processing is controlled at a level above the operating units that use that data.
- *Central Administration of Data* The control of data resides in a single administration function. This results in a concentration of responsibilities.

The computer control strategy for data independence is one of determining control of the organization's data. While it is recognized that all data is the property of the organization, it is the control over the data that determines its usage. If control is at the departmental or user level, that user will share data only after the user's immediate needs are satisfied.

Competency of People

The number, types, and skills of people employed in data processing are an important part of the information system strategy. One organization in the early 1960s decided to hire the best "brainpower" available. It stacked its data processing department with MBA's, computer science majors, and other highly trained people. The result was a great leap forward in the sophistication of the corporation's information systems.

The competency of people is often related to the organization's pay policies. Obviously, all organizations want the most competent people they can attract. However, if a company offers $150 per week for a programmer, it will get a $150-per-week programmer. You may want an extremely able, experienced, and skilled programmer for $150 per week, but the odds are that at that salary range you will be settling for a community college graduate, and probably not one who was at the top of the class.

Management should think through the types of information strategy it can implement with its current level of data processing competency. It would be unrealistic to attempt to install a complex on-line interactive data base system using programmers paid only $150 per week. On the other hand, if the organization can utilize predeveloped application programs, then a $150-per-week programmer may provide all the competency that is needed. Problems occur when the expectations of management exceed the capabilities of the data processing personnel, or vice versa.

The pressure under which people operate also affects their performance. For example, if the data processing staff is continually pressed to perform at an above normal pace or put in overtime on a long-term basis, performance is normally affected adversely. One of the major causes of computer system failures is insufficient time to design, implement, test, or change an application. The low-risk criteria on the competency of people continuum include (see Figure 4.6):

- *High Skills* Data processing personnel possess all the necessary skills.
- *High Training* The organization provides the necessary training to maintain its employees' skills at an up-to-date level.
- *High Integrity* The control climate encourages high morale and loyalty.
- *Sufficient Number of People* There are enough competent people to perform the assigned work in the allotted time.

The criteria indicating a high risk on the competency of people continuum include:

- *Low Skills* Employees' skills are insufficient to do the work assigned.
- *Low Training* Employees do not get training sufficient to maintain their skills.
- *Low Integrity* People are working only to make a living.
- *Insufficient Number of People* There is more work to be performed than can be accomplished in the allotted time.

The computer control strategy regarding the competency of people should attempt to match the sophistication of the systems with the ability of employees. This matching includes hiring people

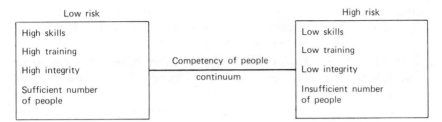

Figure 4.6 **Competency of People.**

with the appropriate skills, providing training to maintain those skills, and hiring a sufficient number of competent people to perform the needed work.

Selection of Computer Technology

One of the most exciting aspects of the computer field is the selection of hardware and software. It is one that is enjoyed by many data processing personnel and is considered prestigious.

Data processing personnel often equate their marketability as data processing professionals with the hardware and software on which they are skilled. If they work in an organization that has an old IBM 1401 computer, their marketability is almost nil. The same is true for hardware and software that is not widely accepted by industry. On the other hand, if they are using the most current hardware and software from a major computer vendor, their skills are extremely marketable.

It is advantageous, therefore, for data processing people to use the most current hardware and software. Management must recognize this in establishing its hardware and software selection strategy.

When new hardware and software first come on the market, there is a high probability they will have problems. The first organizations to use this hardware and software are the ones that spend time and effort trying to detect and correct these problems. For this reason, many organizations have established a policy of not using new hardware and software until a year or more after their first installation elsewhere. Their strategy is to let their competitors pay the cost of debugging new hardware and software.

The criteria that indicate a low risk on the computer technology continuum include (see Figure 4.7):

- *Proven Hardware Technology* The hardware selected has been installed in other organizations for a period of time sufficient to uncover most of the hardware bugs.
- *Proven Software Technology* The software has been installed in enough installations for a period of time sufficient to uncover most software bugs.
- *Upgradable System* The hardware or software can be expanded to provide greater processing capabilities if needed.
- *Proven Vendors* The vendor has a record that indicates it will provide conversion aids to new hardware and software, continually upgrade its product to meet users' increasing needs, and provide timely and adequate service.

The criteria that indicate a high risk on the computer technology continuum include:

- *New Hardware Technology* The hardware has yet to be proven in practice.
- *New Software Technology* The software has yet to be proven in practice.
- *At Upper End of Systems Capabilities* The hardware and/or software cannot be expanded.
- *Unproven Vendors* The vendor lacks one or more desirable characteristics.

The selection strategy for computer technology should be integrated into the long-range systems plan of the organization. In other words, an organization should not change to a new version of an operating system or add additional memory unless it can be shown that this is advantageous to the organization. Without such a strategy,

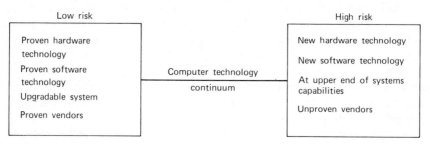

Figure 4.7 **Selection of Computer Technology.**

many organizations find themselves adopting each new release of software with the accompanying disruption in data processing capabilities and with little, if any, payback.

Systems Development Process

In the early 1960s the cost of developing and maintaining systems exceeded the cost of the hardware on which they were run. Today the systems development cost in most organizations exceeds the cost of hardware many times over. As hardware costs continue to drop and labor costs increase, this gap will widen.

Many organizations have experienced the majority of their systems and programming effort being expended on systems maintenance. Some organizations have indicated that up to 80% of their systems and programming effort is expended on maintenance, and only 20% on new systems development. The combination of the labor and maintenance costs highlights the need for improving the systems development process.

During the last 10 years, much effort has been expended on improving the methods of building systems. In the late 1950s and early 1960s it was considered an art to build a computer system. No two systems were alike. Time and experience have shown that there is a great commonality to the process of developing systems.

The concept of the systems development life cycle (SDLC) started an orderly development process that has been expanded through structured design, HIPO (hierarchical input process and output), flowcharting, and structured programming. When sophisticated scheduling systems are added, such as critical path scheduling, the ability of data processing personnel to predict the time and effort to develop systems is becoming extremely precise.

Structured design and structured programming have helped reduce maintenance costs. Using techniques of this type has enabled systems personnel to make changes easily. The maintenance of data independently of processing has also helped reduce the percentage of effort put into maintenance.

Organizations need a systems development strategy. The objective of this strategy is to provide the necessary controls to assure management that systems will be built on time and within the budget and will meet the needs of the users. Without a systems development strategy, systems analysts and programmers are free to select whatever methods they choose in designing systems. Some may be very good, but they may lack the consistency needed to provide high-quality data processing.

The criteria that indicate a low risk on the systems development continuum include (see Figure 4.8):

- *SDLC* Computerized business applications are installed, operated, and maintained according to an orderly method.
- *Standards* Common procedures are used in designing, documenting, programming, testing, operating, and maintaining computer applications.
- *Job Accounting* Records are maintained on the status of implementation, schedules, and budgets.
- *Structured Design* Computer systems are built and specified according to an orderly method.
- *Adequate Documentation* Information is sufficient to ensure continuity of development, operation, and maintenance.

The criteria that indicate a high risk on the systems development continuum include:

- *System Dependent on Quality of People* Lacking standards and procedures, the quality of the system is dependent on the competency of people.
- *Minimal Structure to Design* The design is not tied together in a manner that is easy to maintain.
- *Minimal Monitoring During Design* Management is not involved during the development process to check status and make "go, no go" decisions based on that status. Without such a process,

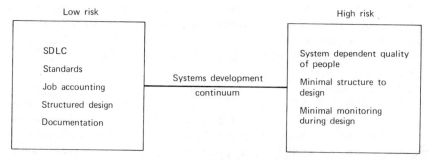

Figure 4.8   **Systems Development Process.**

management is not in a position to abort a poor system until it is operational.

Data Processing Controls

Top management develops corporate control policies and procedures, but much of the day-to-day implementation may be left to the user area. In many organizations there is more concern with achieving objectives than with the methods and controls used to achieve those objectives. Now having adequate internal accounting controls in systems is the law of the land.

The Foreign Corrupt Practices Act of 1977 initiated a need to develop a control strategy. Prior to that, most organizations did not specifically address control from a strategy perspective. Specifying and overseeing control was normally left to the systems analyst or the initiator of the system.

There are three aspects of a system of control. These are design, assessment, and adjustment. Design is often a responsibility shared by the user of the application and the data processing personnel. The assessment is a management function that in many organizations is delegated to auditors. The adjustment of controls is a responsibility shared by the management, the user, and the data processing personnel.

The design of controls should attempt to put into practice the organization's control strategy. The strategy must specify the control process, which the guidelines contained in this book help fulfill.

Since the early 1970s, the presence of auditors in the data processing area has become more prevalent. A whole new specialty group within auditing, called EDP auditing, has evolved. One of the objectives of EDP auditing it to assess the adequacy of internal control. This assessment includes controls over development, as well as over operation. The assessment looks at environmental, application, and operational controls.

Controls are not measurable without standards. For example, if there is no standard requiring programs to be specified before written, there can be no control over that process. Thus there is a close interrelationship between standards and control.

Those people responsible for assessing control perform that assessment by measuring a process against a standard. For example, if there is a policy (i.e., a standard) that requires two signatures on checks of more than $1000, that standard or control can be readily assessed by looking at those checks. If they all have two signatures, the assessor knows the standard has been followed. If the standard has not been followed, then some adjustment must be made in the process to provide management an assurance that the standard will be followed.

The last part of control strategy is the adjustment process. The primary concern here is that when control weaknesses or violations are noted, they will be adequately addressed and corrected on a timely basis if that correction is warranted.

The criteria that indicate a low risk on the EDP controls continuum include (see Figure 4.9):

- *EDP Audits* An independent group assesses the adequacy of implemented controls.
- *Regular Status Reports* Management is continually advised about the status of design, assessments, and adjustments of controls.
- *Quality Control* An independent group provides assurance that systems are designed, implemented, and operated according to data processing standards. In many organizations this is called a quality assurance function.
- *Management Approval Checkpoints* At selected points during systems development and major maintenance efforts, management has the option to stop or alter implementation. This puts management in a position of having control over the use of systems and programming resources.
- *Control Standards* The methods of control have been formalized in, for example, standard tape labels, standard documentation formats, and standard programming notebooks.

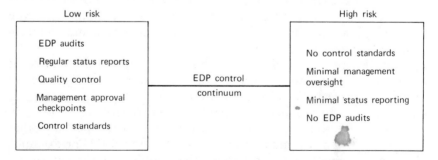

Figure 4.9 **EDP Controls.**

The criteria that indicate a high risk on the EDP control continuum include:

- *No Control Standards*   No predetermined methods for designing controls exist.
- *Minimal Management Oversight*   Management is not personally involved in establishing control policy, assessing control, and ensuring that adjustments are made when needed.
- *Minimal Status Reporting*   Management is not adequately advised about the events occurring in the data processing area.
- *No EDP Audits*   There is no independent assessment of the adequacy of controls in a computerized business environment.

USING COMPUTER CONTROL STRATEGY IN SYSTEMS DESIGN

The risk inherent in the organization's control strategy should be assessed as a part of designing the system of internal controls. This provides the designer of controls with an assessment of risk that can be used to build application controls. It is also used by management to establish environmental controls.

Let's look at how this computer control strategy risk assessment can be used. Let's assume that the strategy for acquiring computer technology was rated as a very high risk, perhaps because the organization had recently acquired some unproven hardware and software. Knowing this, the data processing function could design some controls to reduce the risk associated with the improper use of technology. These controls might be to conduct acceptance tests on the new hardware and software or to require the vendor to provide systems engineering assistance during startup to help isolate problems associated with the new hardware and software. If the systems analyst understands the risks in the computer area, the analyst can use additional control to reduce that risk. If data base controls are weak, for example, the analyst can add extra data integrity controls.

The risk assessment of the information strategy is a subjective judgment. However, by understanding the criteria on which that judgment is made, most senior systems analysts can make a reasonable judgment. These criteria have been outlined in this chapter.

Each of the information strategy areas should be rated on a five-point scale as follows:

- *Very High Risk*   The possibility of loss due to the risks inherent in the selected strategy is very high.
- *High Risk*   There is a high probability that a loss will occur as a result of this strategy unless strong controls are initiated.
- *Average Risk*   The risk appears reasonable based on the organization's strategy.
- *Low Risk*   The strategy, coupled with existing controls, makes the probability of loss low.
- *Very Low Risk*   The probability of loss associated with this strategy is very low. In some cases, this rating indicates that the area may be overcontrolled and thus the controls are not cost-effective.

Exhibit 4.1 is a worksheet that can be used for rating the information strategy areas. Systems analysts can refer to this worksheet when designing controls for a computerized business environment. The areas of high risk warrant increased effort on control, whereas the areas of low risk may require minimal or no additional controls.

Exhibit 4.1   Assessment of the Information Strategy Risk

	Risk				
Information Strategy Area	Very High	High	Average	Low	Very Low
Diversity of data use					
Accessibility of data					
Sharing of business systems					
Data independence					
Competency of people					
Selection of computer technology					
Systems development process					
EDP Controls					

SUMMARY

This chapter has presented an overview of how computer control strategy affects control design. The types of controls that are affected by information strategy are primarily environmental controls. Strategy itself tends to be implemented and enforced at an organizationwide level. The following chapter covers the specific controls needed to achieve the environmental control objectives.

CHAPTER 5

Making Controls Work

Controls work when risk is reduced to an acceptable level. If a user can live with five errors per day of type X and the controls are adequate to contain errors of type X to no more than five per day, the controls are working.

Planning is needed to make controls work; good controls don't just happen. The planning is composed of identifying the risk, establishing an acceptable level of risk, and then building a system of control that will meet those objectives of control.

This chapter outlines a control development life cycle (CDLC). This life cycle is the blueprint for building an effective system of internal control.

An essential element in the information control strategy is management's control attitude. If top management establishes a strong control environment, the probability of implementing an effective system of internal control is substantially increased.

Management's attitude can be illustrated by a computer room situation. Suppose one company in the aerospace industry has a sign inside the computer room door that states, "Failure to expell unauthorized visitors from this room will result in immediate dismissal of all operators present." In one instance when an unauthorized visitor is found in the computer room, all operators are immediately fired. The organization enforced the security control of not permitting unauthorized people in the computer room. However, if in another organization the disclosure of an unauthorized visitor in the computer room only resulted in a slight reprimand, the computer operators would quickly learn that management does not really intend to enforce its controls. In an environment where management is supportive of controls, such as in the first computer room example, it is likely that a system of internal controls will be effective.

CONTROL DEVELOPMENT LIFE CYCLE (CDLC)

The objective of control is to lessen the probability of loss due to business risks. This implies that the risks are identified and a determination is made as to what level of risk is acceptable. Once this is done, an orderly process can be followed in designing controls. After the design, one important aspect of control remains—the continual monitoring and adjustment of controls so that they remain effective.

The two most important criteria in control design are cost-effectiveness and meeting user needs. When controls are not coordinated with user needs and responsibilities, controls lose their effectiveness. A poor control may be worse than no control at all, and poor controls may encourage people to circumvent them.

The cost-effectiveness criterion in designing adequate controls is important because it is the only criterion included in the Foreign Corrupt Practices Act of 1977. According to the act, if a control is needed to adequately control a situation, and the control is cost-effective, it must be implemented.

Controls should be designed using a systems analysis approach. Systems are designed using the SDLC approach and many of the lessons learned in systems design can be applied, creating a CDLC.

The control process, like the systems development process, should be orderly and methodical. Just as systems development proceeds through an SDLC so should control proceed through a CDLC, which includes the following steps:

- Step 1—risk identification.
- Step 2—acceptable (consistent) level of risk determination.
- Step 3—placement of controls.
- Step 4—controls designed to reduce risk to the acceptable (consistent) level.

- Step 5—feedback provision.
- Step 6—feedback information analysis.
- Step 7—control adjustments (needed to assure some acceptable or consistent level of controls is achieved).

The steps should be conducted in sequence (see Figure 5.1). The process begins as the risks are identified and proceeds through the

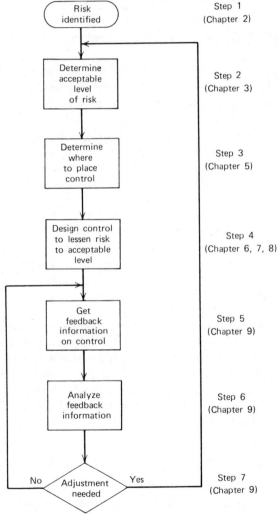

Figure 5.1 **Control Process.**

adjustment or control maintenance step. At that point, controls are changed to ensure continued effectiveness. Too frequently the CDLC ends after the controls have been developed. This is an impractical approach to controls, as impractical as systems development would be if it did not take into account the need for systems maintenance. The following discussion explains each of these life cycle steps.

STEP 1—RISK IDENTIFICATION

Chapter 2 describes the risks in a computerized business environment. These are general risks and should be so considered during the systems design process. As the design becomes more specific, however, so must the description of the risks.

For example, the concentration of data risk is appropriate when discussing the system and the general level of risk. This general risk describes a condition that could result in a loss, but it needs to be broken into specific risks prior to determining the acceptable level of risk. For example, a specific risk associated with the concentration of data would be the loss of data due to a concurrent update of the same data element in an on-line data base environment. In other words, if party A removes item X from the data base to change it, and before it is returned party B, also removes item X to change it, one of the updates will be lost because one of the two parties will place the changed data on top of the other's changed data.

To exhaustively list detailed risks here would be impractical, because there is no commonality to business systems and the risks to which those systems are subjected. For example, it is estimated that there are approximately 50,000 different payroll systems in the United States. If organizations can find 50,000 different ways to perform payroll, they may find 50,000 different specific risks for those systems.

The suggested method to define specific risks for a computerized application is a three-part process. The first part is to consider one of the general risks. The second part is to use interviews and analysis to determine the specific risks. This process involves analysis of what can go wrong in the system being designed. The third part of the process is to determine in which areas the controls should be placed to lessen the risk (i.e., environmental, application, and operational).

Let's review an example of a systems analyst designing a payroll application. The analyst would examine individually all 11 general risks (discussed in Chapter 2). However, because the analyst is only concerned with the application, it may not be necessary to evaluate environmental controls because they apply to all applications and should be developed by management. This assumes the analyst knows what controls exist in the environment. Let's assume the analyst was examining the concentration of data risk. For the application control area, the analyst might list the following as specific concentration of data risks:

- Loss of individual employee rights to privacy.
- Loss of updated information due to multiple concurrent updates.
- Increased loss if data is lost (i.e., all the eggs are in one basket).

The concentration of data also provides an operational risk for which some specific risks are:

- Processing inefficiency due to increased access time.
- Increased cost to maintain backup and recovery information.
- Reduced program efficiency due to large file size.

Once these specific risks have been identified, the analyst is ready to determine an acceptable level of risk.

STEP 2—DETERMINATION OF ACCEPTABLE LEVEL OF RISK

The process for determining an acceptable level of risk, or acceptable level of loss, is described in Chapter 3. This mechanical function is not the difficult part of the process, however. The difficult decisions involve both selecting the risk determinants (i.e., the frequency of loss and average loss per occurrence) and then deciding, if that probable loss is unacceptable, what level of loss is acceptable.

The risk determinants can be most easily decided by first selecting a range of values into which most analysts agree the determinants should fall. For example, rather than picking $1000 as a probable loss, it is better to pick a range, such as $100 to $10,000. Using a range causes less argument and may prove sufficient for determining an acceptable level of loss. In this example, $10,000 might be acceptable. The range can be narrowed by examining the detailed factors that actually affect the value. If the loss in question related to a fire, for example, one could examine the following factors in an effort to narrow the range:

- Value of items that could be destroyed.
- Where items are stored.
- Cost to repair fire-damaged items.
- Fire protection system.
- Insurance coverage.

Determining an acceptable level of loss is a user responsibility. The individual accountable for the loss must ultimately decide how much loss is acceptable. For example, if the loss in question is bad checks, then it must be decided how much of a loss resulting from bad checks is acceptable. If risk analysis projected, based on current processing procedures, a potential loss of $10,000 per year due to bad checks, the individual responsible for bad check losses must decide if $10,000 per year is acceptable or if not, what amount is acceptable. *Unless this step is performed, the specification of controls is delegated to the system analyst/programmer, and the users, delinquent in their responsibility, are not entitled to complain about the results.*

STEP 3—PLACEMENT OF CONTROLS

Controls are normally placed on activities. Risks are ever present and thus cannot be eliminated. For example, the risk of error in entering data is always present. What can be controlled are the activities where those risks are present.

For example, fire is a risk, although one not unique to data processing. It is impossible to control the risk of fire, because fire can occur anywhere at any time, but we can control the risk at the place where fire occurs (i.e., we can control the activity). For example, the computer room is a place where a fire can occur, and when we realize this we can construct fireproof walls, insert a Halon system, put fire extinguishers on the wall, and insert fire alarms. All these controls reduce the probability that the risk of fire will be turned into a loss. To reduce the loss resulting from risks that are unique to or increased in a computerized business environment, we must determine the activities or places where those risks occur. Then we can establish our controls. For example, a concentration of data risk may occur only in centralized data base activities and on- and off-site libraries. Chapters 6, 7, and 8 explain how to select specific controls for such specific cases.

STEP 4—CONTROLS DESIGNED TO REDUCE RISKS
TO THE ACCEPTABLE LEVEL

The acceptable level of risk becomes the control design specification. However, the specification should be positively stated as an objective of control. In addition, which area of control that objective falls into must be determined, as the individual control techniques vary depending on the control area.

The three areas of control in a computerized business environment are illustrated in Figure 5.2. These are the environmental, application, and operational control areas. In a computerized business environment, these areas of control are influenced by the information strategy of the organization.

Environmental controls are controls that affect all systems in the organization. Application controls are normally transaction-oriented controls and thus tend to be restricted to a specific application, such as balancing the detail accounts receivable records with the control totals. Operational controls are designed to ensure the effectiveness, economy, and efficiency of operations, for example the job accounting system software records usage of system resources.

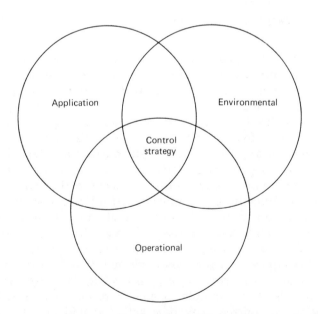

Figure 5.2   **Three Areas of Control.**

ENVIRONMENTAL CONTROLS

The environment establishes the methods and procedures by which work can be performed. Environmental controls are normally the policies, procedures, and standards to be followed when performing the work. They are independent of any individual application. In an automated environment, some of these controls are automated; but many environmental controls are manual administrative procedures. The environmental control objectives are security, integrity, availability, and recovery. These control objectives are selected to emphasize the environmental areas needing control, but are consistent with those published by the major accounting associations.

Environmental controls govern both resources and activities. The data availability and recovery control objectives involve the data processing resources, whereas the control objectives of security and integrity involve activities.

Security Control Objective

Control over the security of information is the key building block of control. If management cannot be assured that data is adequately protected (i.e., only authorized access to that data is permitted), it can place very little reliance on any other control. For example, if it is possible to access data without detection, a person can perform unauthorized operations that are almost impossible to detect. The vulnerabilities an organization faces when it does not provide adequate security controls include the following, all of which are unauthorized acts:

- *Lack of Detection* Someone can remove information or assets without detection.
- *Compromise* The confidentiality of data is lost.
- *Loss of Privacy* Individual rights may be compromised.
- *Accessibility* People and/or systems can access data to which they are not authorized.

The objective of security control is to ensure that all data processing activity is authorized by preventing, detecting, and responding to unauthorized access.

Integrity Control Objective

The integrity of the environment provides assurance that data, once authorized and accurately entered, will not be changed through an unintentional act. While security deals primarily with accessibility, integrity deals with the soundness of data. Integrity controls are those controls that ensure the correctness of the processes (i.e., they are accurate, complete, and timely). If an organization does not provide sufficient integrity controls, it is vulnerable to the following:

- *Modification* Data may be changed erroneously in an unintentional manner.
- *Destruction* Data may be lost by an unintentional act.
- *Inadequate Audit Trail* The organization may not be able to reconstruct processing (activity) to substantiate the accuracy and completeness of data.

Availability Control Objective

The value of data is having it available when and where needed. The current emphasis on distributed processing, and on-line interactive systems, is to get data where it is needed, when it is needed. Therefore, an organization may be threatened by the following problems if it does not provide adequate availability controls:

- *Temporary Loss* The needed information cannot be located.
- *Untimely Delivery* The information cannot be provided at the time it is needed.
- *Inadequate Service Level* The computing resources are inadequate to meet one or more user needs.

Recovery Control Objective

The reliance on computers and computer media requires the capability to recover operations after a problem is encountered, and the objective of the recovery control is to ensure an eventual recovery from failure. The centralization of information increases the importance of this control objective. Also, as systems become more integrated and produce less hard copy information, organizations must rely on machine-readable data as their official organization records.

An organization faces the following vulnerabilities when it does not provide effective recovery controls:

- *Data Not Retained* Information is not retained, and no means are provided to reconstruct that data.
- *Processing Facility Inoperable* Information cannot be retrieved or processed because the needed processing facility is not available.
- *Key People Lost* The skills needed to obtain, process, or modify information are unavailable.

Need for Environmental Controls

Adequate environmental controls provide a climate in which application controls are encouraged and effective (See Exhibit 5.1.) In manual systems, application controls assume the greater importance in information processing. However, as computer systems assume

Exhibit 5.1 Environmental Control Objectives

Control Objective	Vulnerability
Security	Lack of detection
	Compromise
	Loss of privacy
	Accessibility
Integrity	Modification
	Destruction
	Inadequate audit trail
Availability	Temporary loss
	Untimely delivery
	Inadequate service level
Recovery	Data not retained
	Processing facility inoperable
	Key people lost

more functions, there is a migration of control from the application to the environment. In early computer applications security was primarily an application control objective. For example, the payroll department may have used a special vault in which to lock payroll information. In a data base system this is not practical, and security must be controlled for all applications using the data base. Thus security becomes an environmental control as opposed to an application control. However, the responsibility for the application data remains with the application.

APPLICATION CONTROLS

Application control objectives are primarily activity-related controls to ensure achievement of data-oriented objectives. These controls govern the accuracy, completeness, consistency, and authorization of data. They are normally designed for a specific application, such as payroll, accounts recievable, or demand deposits accounts.

Application controls oversee the processing of data from its origination through its use. In a computerized business application, some controls are manual, while others are automated. Some of the controls are under the direction of the data processing department, and others are under the direction of those preparing and using data.

Completeness Control Objective

The completeness of data is assurance that all the necessary data has been entered into the application. This includes more than a concern with lost and misplaced data; it involves placing data into the appropriate accounting period. Many of the more serious EDP problems involve the placement of data in the wrong accounting period. Inadequate completeness controls may force an organization to confront the following vulnerabilities:

- *Omissions* Data that should be included is not.
- *Misclassification* Data is inappropriately coded so that it does not appear in the proper account or application (i.e., improper accounting).
- *Cutoffs* Data is recorded in the wrong accounting period.

Accuracy Control Objective

The accurate recording of data means that the individual data elements in a transaction properly reflect the event that has occurred. For example, if five tires have been ordered, the order should reflect five tires. The vulnerabilities an organization faces when adequate accuracy controls are not provided include:

- *Data Error* The data is incorrect.
- *Misrepresentation* Data is changed so that is no longer reflects the actual occurrence (e.g., the recorded sale amount includes both the purchase price and tax).
- *Error of Omission* The data does not reflect the actual event that occurred (e.g., a political contribution is recorded as a legal expense).

Consistency Control Objective

People using information need to understand the framework in which that information was gathered and processed. If two or more parties use the same information, that information should reflect the same reliability and timeliness. For example, if the pay of two employees is being compared, the pay should be consistently reported, such as in the amount of normal weekly pay. Without consistency, the average weekly pay of one employee might be compared to the actual pay dollars another employee received in one particular pay period. This leads to inconsistent results. The following vulnerabilities may endanger an organization if it does not provide adequate consistency controls:

- *Unreliable Data* The user of data cannot rely on the data.
- *Uncomparable Data* Data from two sources cannot be compared.
- *Data Not Reported According to Generally Accepted Accounting Principles* There are generally accepted accounting principles that apply to the recording and reporting of data. If data is not processed according to these procedures, accountants cannot interpret the proper meaning of the data.
- *Data Not Fairly Presented* The data presented may not fairly represent what actually happened.

Authorization Control Objective

Data entered into systems should be authorized and transacted in accordance with the policies and procedures of management. One of the provisions of the U.S. Foreign Corrupt Practices Act of 1977 is just that: transactions are to be processed in accordance with management's intents. Prior to recording data, controls should ascertain that the data is authorized. If authorization controls are inadequate and organization may face the following vulnerabilities:

- *Invalid Data*   Data that is not proper is entered and processed.
- *Management Policy Violated*   Transactions that violate management policy are processed. Even seemingly authorized transactions may violate management policy. For example, an individual may buy an unauthorized item by purchasing it in component pieces.

Exhibit 5.2   Application Control Objectives

Control Objective	Vulnerability
Completeness	Omissions
	Misclassification
	Cutoffs
Accuracy	Data Error
	Misrepresentations
	Error of commission
Consistency	Unreliable data
	Uncomparable data
	Data not reported to generally accepted accounting principles
	Data not fairly presented
Authorization	Invalid data
	Management policy violated
	Illegal transaction
	Unethical transaction

- *Illegal Transaction* The transaction violates one or more laws.
- *Unethical Transaction* The transaction is not in the best interest of the organization and may be a conflict of interest.

See Exhibit 5.2 for a summary of application control objectives.

OPERATIONAL CONTROLS

Most discussions of controls stop after environmental and application controls have been discussed. However, for the purpose of understanding and applying controls in a computerized business environment, a third category, operational controls, needs to be considered. It is through these operational controls that management exercises direction over the effectiveness, efficiency, economy of operation, and the satisfaction of user needs.

One of the least recognized objectives of control is control over the operational performance of an organization. Most successful organizations translate their formula for success into operational practices that include controls. For example, if certain computer techniques, such as blocking factors, are found to maximize the use of a tape or disk drive, they are turned into standards and controlled.

One of the most discouraging moments in a computer professional's life is to build an efficient, effective, and economical application that nobody wants. To misinterpret and implement unwanted needs has caused many people to leave their positions out of frustration. Controls can help avoid this dilemma.

Operational control objectives help ensure that user needs are met in an efficient, economical, and effective manner. These operational control objectives are selected to emphasize the operational areas needing control. Many of these controls can be automated.

Efficiency Control Objectives

Efficiency in the performance of work means expending the least amount of effort necessary to accomplish the job. Sometimes it is not practical to search out the most efficient method of accomplishing the job, but efficiency should always be an objective. As people learn how to perform tasks more efficiently, they should incorporate those methods into standards and procedures. The vulnerabilities an organization faces there is no provision for adequate efficiency controls include:

- *Over Budget* Projects are not completed within the allocated funds.
- *Not on Schedule* Projects are not completed within the allocated time.
- *Accountability* Assignments of responsibilities and authorities are not consistent with the organizational structure and personnel capabilities.

Effectiveness Control Objective

The effectiveness of an operation relates to the accomplishment of the stated objectives. Providing the needed information, in the right format and delivered to the right place on time, means successful accomplishment of the mission. Being effective does not necessarily mean that the task is performed efficiently or economically. However, most users rate effectiveness higher than efficiency and economy. Inadequate effectiveness controls may cause an organization to face the following vulnerabilities:

- *Misuse of People* People are required to do extra work because the system fails to meet their objectives.
- *Misuse of Technology* Tasks that might be accomplished are not because the hardware and software are not properly utilized.
- *Inadequate Control Strategy* The control strategy is not be able to minimize the probability of occurrence (preventive control) or the impact of occurrence (easy detection and prompt corrective action).

Economy Control Objective (Cost/Benefit of Controls)

Systems should be performed in the most ecnomical manner possible. This does not always mean that the most economical use can be made of every aspect of the system. For example, the total system may be more economical when higher-level computer languages are used, even though they utilize more computer time than would be expended by using a lower-level language. The vulnerabilities an organization faces when it does not provide adequate economy controls include:

- *Improper Use of Technology* The process of developing, operating, and maintaining computerized applications utilizes excess resources.
- *Not Cost/Beneficial* The control being used is not cost/beneficial with respect to either time or cost from a capital investment perspective or from the operational impact over the application's useful life. The questions that need to be asked are:
  - Is this control cost-effective?
  - Is this control a cost of doing business (i.e., required by law, the Internal Revenue Service, the Securities and Exchange Commission)?

Meets User Needs Control Objective

The primary objective of a computerized application is to satisfy the actual needs of the users of that application. Actual needs are often different from stated needs. If the system fails to meet these actual needs, it has not fulfilled its purpose. Many times actual needs are not fulfilled because systems analysts and users do not communicate effectively or because users of computers do not understand the capabilities that the equipment has for fulfilling their needs. Without adequate controls to help ensure that the users' actual needs are met, an organization faces the following vulnerabilities:

- *Obsolete System* Systems fail to keep pace with changing needs.
- *Wrong Problem Solved* The systems analysts misinterpret the problem to be solved on the computer.

The control objectives and their vulnerabilities are illustrated in Exhibit 5.3.

STEP 5—FEEDBACK PROVISION

Management must continually assess the adequacy of control. This is accomplished by providing management with feedback informa-

Exhibit 5.3   Operational Control Objectives

Control Objective	Vulnerability
Efficiency	Over budget
	Not on schedule
	Accountability
Effectiveness	Misuse of people
	Misuse of technology
	Inadequate control strategy
Economy	Improper use of technology
	Not cost/beneficial
Meets user needs	Obsolescence
	Wrong problem solved

tion on the functioning of the controls. In a previous example we talked of lessening the keystroke error rate from one error per 2000 keystrokes to one per 1000. If key verifying was the control added to lessen that risk, management should monitor the adequacy of that control. In other words, they should monitor the number of keystroke errors per 1000. If it is one per 1000 keystrokes, then the control is functioning properly. However, if the keystroke errors are one per 4000 strokes, then perhaps the controls are too stringent; on the other hand, if the keystroke errors are over one per 1000 keystrokes, additional controls should be added. Feedback information is covered in Chapter 9.

STEP 6—FEEDBACK INFORMATION ANALYSIS

The analysis of feedback information determines whether the controls are adequate. The analysis tells whether the acceptable level of risk is being exceeded, achieved, or not met. This analysis process is discussed in Chapter 9.

STEP 7—CONTROL ADJUSTMENTS

Management should review the analysis and decide whether controls need to be adjusted. If controls are not adjusted when needed, their effectiveness diminishes. Chapter 9 explains this adjustment process.

WHY ARE CONTROLS NEEDED?

If things worked exactly as they should, controls would not be necessary. It is important to have controls only when things can go wrong. So long as Murphy's law exists (i.e., if things can go wrong, they will go wrong), controls will be necessary.

Management has four major responsibilities. These are to organize, plan, direct, and control. It is through control that management is assured that its organization, planning, and directing works.

When management makes a decision regarding the operation of the organization, it has, in effect, established a control objective. Some of the more important controls established by management to achieve control objectives are the organizational structure, the delegation of authority through job description, the preparation of annual budgets, the development of administrative procedures, and the policies for conduct at work. Examples of specific controls on working are hours of work, sickness, and vacation policies. All the controls help assure management that the organization functions according to its desires and intents.

In today's business environment the government imposes a need for control in organizations and establishes requirements for them. To ensure compliance with those laws, management establishes controls. For example, organizations are required under the Federal Wage and Hour Law to pay nonexempt employees time and a half for work over 40 hours per week. To ensure that this law is followed, management classifies workers to isolate those who fall under this law and then maintains records regarding hours worked.

Many laws are beginning to affect the design and operation of computerized business applications. Some of these have a direct effect, others an indirect effect. With the current mood of government being to control business, it seems logical to expect more regulations that affect computers and computerized applications

One of the most significant acts passed by Congress in recent years

Exhibit 5.4   Internal Accounting Control Provisions of the Foreign Corrupt
Practices Act of 1977

For companies subject to the Securities Exchange Act of 1934, the Accounting
Standards Provisions of the act require that they keep, in reasonable detail,
"books, records, and accounts" that accurately and fairly reflect the company's transactions and dispositions of assets; your company must also maintain a system of internal accounting controls providing "reasonable assurances"
that:

(i) transactions are executed in accordance with management's general or
specific authorization;

(ii) transactions are recorded as necessary (I) to permit preparation of
financial statements in conformity with generally accepted accounting
principles or any other criteria applicable to such statements, and (II) to
maintain accountability for assets;

(iii) access to assets is permitted only in accordance with management's
general or specific authorization; and

(iv) the recorded accountability for assets is compared with the existing
assets at reasonable intervals and appropriate action is taken with respect
to any differences.

---

is the Foreign Corrupt Practices Act of 1977. Included within this
act is a provision requiring organizations to maintain an "adequate"
system of internal accounting control. The internal accounting control provisions of this regulation (see Exhibit 5.4) were taken directly
from the professional literature of the AICPA. Thus the accountants'
definition of internal accounting control was written into law for
management adherence.

It is now the law of the land that organizations have an adequate
system of internal accounting control. Because most accounting systems are computerized, this law affects the adequacy of control in
those computerized business applications. Control covers both
the computerized and the manual segments of business applications.

Because under the Foreign Corrupt Practices Act management is
held personally responsible for the adequacy of control, management
probably will be paying more attention to control. Most large organizations are already experiencing the effect of the act. As the Securities and Exchange Commission begins action against companies for
violations, the need for control will be increased.

An example of possible violation of the internal accounting control provisions of the Foreign Corrupt Practices Act is the presence

of a large fourth quarter inventory adjustment. If an organization requires a large inventory adjustment, it can be charged that its system of internal accounting control is inadequate. Therefore, controls in inventory systems should be sufficient to prevent the need for large adjustments.

There are numerous state and federal laws dealing with privacy of computer data. These vary widely from state to state. Privacy laws regulate such things as how long data on employees can be retained and an employee's right to see that data.

Currently, legislation on computer crime is pending. However, this is but one of many bills being considered at the federal and state level regarding the use and misuse of computerized business applications.

Each time a new federal or state law on the use and misuse of computers is passed, new controls must be established. Management and data processing personnel need to stay abreast of these ever-changing and expanding laws.

Regulated industries have specialized laws dealing with their transactions. For example, the controller of the currency has issued many regulations concerning the use of computers in banking.

Computer Data Is Official Data

The computerization of accounting records established a new source of official accounting information. In 1964 the Internal Revenue Service recognized and began to govern the use of computer data as a source of accounting information.

The Internal Revenue Service at that time established five guidelines for computerized applications. These were (see Figure 5.3 for more information):

1. General and subsidiary books of account should be kept. If computerized, the computerized information must support the books of account.
2. Supporting documents and audit trail must be identifiable.
3. Data should be recorded or reconstructable. Audit trails must trace from transactions to totals and from totals to source transactions.
4. Adequate record retention facilities must be maintained.
5. EDP systems must be adequately documented.

26 CFR 601.105: Examination of returns and claims for refund, credit or abatement; determination of correct tax liability.

(Also Part I, Section 6001; 1.6001-1.)

> Guidelines for record requirements to be followed in cases where part or all of the accounting records are maintained within automatic data processing systems.

Section 1. Purpose.

.01 The purpose of this Revenue Procedure is to set forth guidelines specifying the basic record requirements which the Internal Revenue Service considers to be essential in cases where a taxpayer's records are maintained within an automatic data processing (ADP) system. References here to ADP systems include all accounting systems which process all or part of a taxpayer's transactions, records, or data by other than manual methods.

.02 The technology of automatic data processing is evolving rapidly; new methods and techniques are constantly being devised and adopted. Accordingly, the five points set forth in section 4 of this Revenue Procedure are not intended to restrict or prevent taxpayers from obtaining the maximum benefits of ADP provided the appropriate information is present or can be produced by the system. These guidelines will be modified and amended as the need indicates to keep pace with developments in automatic data processing systems.

Sec. 2. Background.

The inherent nature of ADP is such that it may not be possible to trace transactions from source documents to end results or to reconstruct a given account unless the system is designed to provide audit trails. Taxpayers already using ADP or contemplating its use have requested information concerning the types of records that should be developed and maintained in order to meet the requirements of section 6001 of the Internal Revenue Code of 1954 and the corresponding regulations. This section of the Code reads in part as follows:

Every person liable for any tax imposed by this title, or for the collection thereof, shall keep such records, render such statements, make such returns, and comply with such rules and regulations as the Secretary or his delegate may from time to time prescribe * * *

Sec. 3. Objectives.

Modern machine accounting systems are capable of recording business transactions much more rapidly and with greater accuracy than manual systems and they are capable of retaining and producing vast amounts of data. The ability to produce in legible form the data necessary to determine at a later date whether or not the correct tax li- negligible in comparison to the expense that may be incurred at a later date if the system cannot practically and readily provide the infor-

Figure 5.3 Internal Revenue Service Procedure 64-12.

mation needed to support and substantiate the accuracy of the previously reported tax liability.

Sec. 4. ADP Record Guidelines.

.01 ADP accounting systems will vary, just as manual systems vary, from taxpayer to taxpayer. However, the procedures built into a computer's accounting program must include a method of producing from the punched cards or tapes visible and legible records which will provide the necessary information for the verification of the taxpayer's tax liability.

.02 In determining the adequacy of records maintained within an automatic data processing system, the Service will consider as acceptable those systems that comply with the guidelines for record requirements as follows:

(1) *General and Subsidiary Books of Account.*—A general ledger, with source references, should be written out to coincide with financial reports for tax reporting periods. In cases where subsidiary ledgers are used to support the general ledger accounts, the subsidiary ledgers should also be written out periodically.

(2) *Supporting Documents and Audit Trail.*—The audit trail should be designed so that the details underlying the summary accounting data, such as invoices and vouchers, may be identified and made available to the Internal Revenue Service upon request.

(3) *Recorded or Reconstructible Data.*—The records must provide the opportunity to trace any transaction back to the original source or forward to a final total. If printouts are not made of transactions at the time they are processed, then the system must have the ability to reconstruct these transactions.

(4) *Data Storage Media.*—Adequate record retention facilities must be available for storing tapes and printouts as well as all applicable supporting documents. These records must be retained in accordance with the provisions of the Internal Revenue Code of 1954 and the regulations prescribed thereunder.

(5) *Program Documentation.*—A description of the ADP portion of the accounting system should be available. The statements and illustrations as to the scope of operations should be sufficiently detailed to indicate (a) the application being performed, (b) the procedures employed in each application (which, for example, might be supported by flow charts, block diagrams or other satisfactory descriptions of input or output procedures), and (c) the controls used to insure accurate and reliable processing. Important changes, together with their effective dates, should be noted in order to preserve an accurate chronological record.

Sec. 5. Comments or Inquiries.

Comments or inquiries relating to this Revenue Procedure should be addressed to the Assistant Commissioner (Compliance), Attention: CP:A, Washington, D.C., 20224.

Figure 5.3 (continued)

Section 6001.—Notice or Regulations Requiring Records, Statements, and Special Returns

26 CFR 1.6001-1: Records.

Punched cards, magnetic tapes, disks, and other machine-sensible data media used in the automatic data processing of accounting transactions constitute records within the meaning of section 1.6001-1 of the regulations.

Rev. Rul. 71-20 [1]

Advice has been requested whether punched cards, magnetic tapes, disks, and other machine-sensible data media used in the automatic data processing of accounting transactions constitute records within the meaning of section 6001 of the Internal Revenue Code of 1954 and section 1.6001-1 of the Income Tax Regulations.

In the typical situation the taxpayer maintains records within his automatic data processing (ADP) system. Daily transactions are recorded on punched cards and processed by the taxpayer's computer which prints daily listings and accumulates the individual transaction records for a month's business on magnetic tapes. At the month's end the tapes are used to print out monthly journals, registers, and subsidiary ledgers and to prepare account summary totals entered on punched cards. The summary data from these cards is posted to the general ledger and a monthly printout is generated to reflect opening balances, summary total postings, and closing balances. At the year's end several closing ledger runs are made to record adjusting entries. In other situations taxpayers use punched cards, disks, or other machine-sensible data media to store accounting information.

Section 6001 of the Code provides that every person liable for any tax imposed by the Code, or for the collection thereof, shall keep such records as the Secretary of the Treasury or his delegate may from time to time prescribe.

Section 1.6001-1(a) of the Income Tax Regulations provides that any person subject to income tax shall keep such permanent books of account or records, including inventories, as are sufficient to establish the amount of gross income, deductions, credits, or other matters required to be shown by such person in any return of such tax.

Section 1.6001-1(e) of the regulations provides that the books and records required by this section shall be retained so long as the contents thereof may become material in the administration of any internal revenue law.

It is held that punched cards, magnetic tapes, disks, and other machine-sensible data media used for recording, consolidating, and summarizing accounting transactions and records within a taxpayer's automatic data processing system are records within the meaning of section 6001 of the Code and section 1.6001-1 of the regulations and are required to be retained so long as the contents may become material in the administration of any internal revenue law.

However, where punched cards are used merely as a means of input to the system and the information is duplicated on magnetic tapes, disks, or other machine-sensible records, such punched cards need not be retained.

It is recognized that ADP accounting systems will vary from taxpayer to taxpayer and, usually, will be designed to fit the specific needs of the taxpayer. Accordingly, taxpayers who are in doubt as to which records are to be retained or who desire further information should contact their District Director for assistance.

See Revenue Procedure 64-12, C.B. 1964-1 (Part 1), 672, which sets forth guidelines for keeping records within an ADP system.

---

[1] Also released as Technical Information Release 1062, dated December 31, 1970.

Figure 5.4 Internal Revenue Service Ruling 71-20.

In 1971 the Internal Revenue Service officially recognized computer records as the official records of the organization. As such, organizations were required to retain these records to support tax returns. The Internal Revenue Service issued Ruling 71–20, which outlined the requirements to maintain punched cards, magnetic tapes, disks, and other machine-sensible data media used in the automatic data processing of accounting transactions. This means that all data processing records must be maintained, except when an agreement has been made with the Internal Revenue Service regarding the destruction of machine-sensible data media. Confusion still exists about compliance with this ruling (see Figure 5.4 for more information).

SUMMARY

The objective of control in a computerized business environment is to assist in fulfilling the objectives of the organization. Controls help direct those operations, as well as verify adherence to the intents of management and to government laws and regulations.

Internal control has been defined as:

The plan of organization and all of the coordinate methods and measures adopted within a business to safeguard its assets, check the accuracy and reliability of its accounting data, promote operational efficiency, and encourage adherence to prescribed management policies. This definition possibly is broader than the meaning sometimes attributed to the term. It recognizes that a "system" of internal control extends beyond those matters which relate directly to the functions of the accounting and financial departments.[2]

Accountants have divided internal control into environmental and accounting components. Environmental controls include the plan of organization and the methods and procedures governing the processing of transactions. Environmental controls are designed to ensure that the organization functions according to the intents of management. Accounting controls relate directly to the safeguarding of assets and the reliability of the financial records.

[2] Statement on Auditing Standards," American Institute of Certified Public Accountants, New York, 1973, Section 320.09.

Building a Strong Control Environment

The control environment is strengthened by improving computer control strategies. The recommended approach is to identify the risk (Chapters 2, 3, and 5), determine which control strategy is best suited to reduce the risk, and then select controls adaptable to that strategy. This chapter covers that process for building a strong control environment.

The control environment establishes employee control attitudes. Part of the environment is the controls themselves and part is management's attitude toward control. Attitude is intangible but essential. Employees normally will do what management wants, and if management *emphasizes* and *enforces* control, it will be strong.

This chapter discusses environmental controls, not control attitude. We know how to design and implement controls; we don't know how to make management emphasize and enforce control. However, the Foreign Corrupt Practices Act has forced management to be interested in control, so the opportunity to influence management's control attitude is greater today than it ever has been.

Systems designers implement controls to reduce the probability of loss due to risks. Controls can be placed in either the environment or in the application. If risks apply to all applications, controls should be placed in the environment. However, if risks are confined to a single application, the controls to lessen those risks should be placed in the application.

Four control objectives are normally best accomplished in the environment. These are security, integrity, availability, and recovery procedures. These objectives control the environment in which data is processed, as opposed to the accuracy, completeness, and authorization of the data itself.

The differences between a computerized and noncomputerized environment cause new and increased risks. The computer control strategy of an organization is developed to deal with these differences. Controls incorporated into the strategy are normally most effective in reducing these new and increased risks when they are part of the environment.

This chapter shows how to design environmental controls using the following:

- Differences between a computerized and noncomputerized environment.
- Risks unique to and increased in a computerized business environment.
- Organizations' computer control strategy.
- Environmental control objectives.

Understanding the interrelationship of these four control considerations will help systems designers place controls at the most cost-effective control points. Systems designers also need to understand the interrelationship, or compensation relationship, between individual controls.

COMPENSATING CONTROL CONCEPTS

The objective of a control is to reduce the risk of loss. Rarely is this done with a single control; more often it is achieved with a combination of controls.

Frequently controls designed to prevent one risk are equally effective against other risks. For example, in an automobile there is a risk of fire and a risk of injury. The steel frame of the automobile is effective against both risks. A reinforced gasoline tank is effective against both risks. The seat belt is not effective against the risk of fire, but is effective against the risk of injury. However, most of the controls built to lessen the loss of injury in an accident are effective against fire. Thus a control in one area may compensate for the lack of controls in another area.

The compensating control concept states that the totality of controls must be considered when determining whether a specific risk is properly controlled. In our previous example, we noted that some controls to lessen the probability of injury from an accident were also effective against fire. If car designers approach controls from a risk perspective and first design controls to lessen injury, they would next determine whether additional controls are needed to lessen the risk of fire. In this instance, controls against injury may compensate for not building controls against fire.

The compensating control concept is very important in the design of controls. If it is ignored, the cost of controls may be increased. The result would be a redundancy of controls, which in many cases is not necessary.

Systems designers should look for the best point in a system to place controls. These are the points where controls can be most cost-effective. They are normally associated with the point in the system where the risk is the greatest and thus the need for control the highest.

ACHIEVING ENVIRONMENTAL CONTROL OBJECTIVES

Controls incorporated into strategy reduce risks. The dilemma facing systems analysts is where to place those specific controls. For example, if we want an effective control strategy for the diversity of data use, where should controls be placed to reduce the risk of inadequate assignment of responsibilities? One more design step is needed for placing a control—finding the specific activity in which to place that control.

The environmental control objectives are placed with the four environmental resources and activities. Security is an activity of protecting the applications and application data. Integrity is an activity designed to ensure the correctness of data. Availability is a resource that provides data to programs and people who need the data. Recovery is a resource to ensure that operations can be successfully restarted after a problem and is also used to sbustantiate the integrity of processing prior to restarting the system.

For each of the four activities, or control objectives, a two-part matrix is provided to aid in placing controls. The first part shows the interrelationship between the risks and the information strategies related to that activity. This part of the matrix is designed to show the areas where control is most needed. The areas in high need of control are indicated with a 3, a 2 indicates an average need for control, and a 1 indicates a low need for control. The systems analyst should be specifically looking for those areas in high need of control.

The second part of the matrix shows the interrelationship of the differences between a computerized and noncomputerized environment and the information strategy. Where the difference has an impact on the strategy, it is indicated by a check in the matrix intersection.

These matrices should be used to:

- Identify the control objective (i.e., activity or resource) where controls are needed.
- Determine which strategies have a high need for control (i.e., those rated a 3) for each activity risk.
- Find the differences that affect control for the activities to be controlled; refer to the differences section of the matrix and find the differences associated with the strategy in which the controls will be placed. These differences will indicate the type of strategy needed.
- Design controls around the differences that will lessen the risks for the strategies indicating a high need for control.
- Determine for each of the strategies whether the designed controls will compensate for the lack of controls in the other strategy areas.
- Determine where to place additional controls if the controls in one area do not adequately compensate for the lack of controls in another strategy area. Controls should then be added in those strategy areas to accommodate the differences.

PLACING SECURITY CONTROLS

Security over the computerized business environment includes both physical and logical security. Physical security covers the computing facilities and related assets and is the responsibility of the data processing manager. Logical security includes protection of the information contained in the organization's files and is the responsibility of the user (i.e., the individual accountable for the data).

Need for Security Controls

Information is one of the most valuable organizational resources. As such, it requires protection. The amount of protection is dependent on the value and the concentration of information. The accessibility of that data, both physically and by communication lines, will determine the emphasis on physical and/or logical controls.

Controls to Reduce Risks

Two risks unique to or increased in a computerized business environment affecting security are concentration of data and concentration of responsibilities. Designing controls to reduce the probabilities of loss due to these two risks provides management the needed assurance of adequate security over the computerized business environment. Examples of the types of controls needed to reduce these risks are discussed, explaining which strategies need controlling, together with examples of controls that might be included with those strategies to reduce the indicated risk (see Exhibit 6.1). The following risks show examples that can be built into the control strategies, which have been indicated on Exhibit 6.1 as the ones where controls are most needed and thus most effective.

Reducing the Concentration of Data Risk. This risk can be reduced by placing controls in the data independence and EDP control information strategy areas. Having a strategy for data independence requires a data base environment. If an organization does not use data base, it should concentrate its efforts on the EDP control strategy.

1. **Improving Data Independence Strategy Control** The control for a data independence strategy is designed to neutralize the automation of control, centralization of functions, new methods of automation, and new processing concepts differences. An effective control is the *security profile (logical security)*, a profile maintained on each user of data indicating what data he or she can access and for what purposes. For example, it can restrict access to the rate field for payroll purposes to read only and, if desired, further restrict the read only capability to weekly pay rates of less than $400 per week.

Exhibit 6.1 Placing Security Controls Matrix

	Control Strategy					
	Diversity of Data Use	Sharing of Business Systems	Data Independence	Selection of Computer Technology	Systems Development Process	EDP Control
EDP Risks[a]						
Concentration of data	1	1	3	1	2	3
Concentration of responsibilities	2	3	1	1	1	3
Differences[b]						
Human functions replaced with machines				√	√	√
Automation of control	√	√	√	√	√	√
Centralization of functions	√	√	√	√	√	√
New methods of authorization			√	√	√	√
New processing concepts			√	√	√	√

[a] 3 = high need for control, 2 = average need for control, 1 = low need for control.
[b] √ = difference affects control.

2. **Improving EDP Control Strategy Control** The EDP control strategy should be designed to ensure proper security over the concentration of data risk. These controls should be designed using the differences involved in this strategy. The differences include the replacement of human functions with machines, automation of control, centralization of functions, and new methods of authorization. Examples of the types of controls that are effective include:

- *Log of Security Abuses (Logical Security)* A log shows the number of security violations detected in an on-line application and the terminal where those unauthorized accesses occurred.
- *Automatic Shutdown (Physical Security)* The terminal is shut down after X number of invalid attempts to gain access to data. Normally a supervisor is required to reopen the terminal.
- *Log of Data Uses (Physical Security)* A log indicates who accessed which data element and for what purposes. It should also show before and after images when the data has been altered. This log can be used to identify who performed what act.

Reducing the Concentration of Responsibilities Risk. Responsibilities are concentrated when multiple users share common data. For sharing to be effective, the users involved must relinquish certain controls to a centralized authority. This involves concentrating control from many areas into a central function or person, which poses the threat of data manipulation. The sharing of business systems and EDP control strategies are the proper points for control to reduce this risk. The following are the strategies best suited to reduce the risk.

1. **Improving Sharing of Business System Strategy Control** Until there is a sharing of business systems, there is little increased risk of concentration of responsibilities. Even using the data base concept does not increase the risk of concentration of responsibilities until two or more users begin sharing the business systems. Controls should be designed to compensate for the differences associated with automation of control and centralization of functions. These concentrate responsibilities into the data base administration function. Controls effective in this strategy include:

- *Data Administrator* A high-level corporate officer or manager has the responsibility of overseeing and coordinating information systems processing for the organization. The data administrator establishes information policies on such things as use, definition, security, timeliness, and so on.
- *User Signoffs* The users in this shared responsibilities environment sign a statement indicating that they have reviewed and concur with the agreed upon methods of operation. This can be done at checkpoints during development or just prior to implementation.

2. **Improving EDP Control Strategy Control** The objective of EDP control strategy is assurance that the other functions are working. Some controls that help lessen the concentration of responsibilities risk include:

- *Audits* An unannounced independent review of the concentrated responsibilities can be used to identify potential control weaknesses.
- *User Redundancy Controls* User controls are maintained to duplicate computer controls, such as independently maintaining a cash receipts total and then manually comparing it to the cash applied to the accounts receivable system.

PLACING AVAILABILITY CONTROLS

The activity of making data available to users ranges from a simple tape mount in a tape batched environment to a potentially complex retrieval system in an on-line data base environment. Needed data comes from both normal computer-produced outputs and special inquiries. If all the data needed is together in one file, the retrieval process is normally quite simple. For example, if a credit manager wants to know the outstanding balance of a particular customer, that information should be readily available. On the other hand, if the credit manager wants to know the three-year payment history of a particular customer, that information might be difficult to obtain. Availability also depends on the type of inquiry tools available to gather information.

Need for Availability Controls

Information systems are valuable only when they provide the needed information. The right information must be made available to the right user at the right time. Not having the information when needed is the result of the risks of the improper use of technology and the inability to control technology. If the user does not have the needed information on a timely basis, then the user is not able to react quickly to business situations. Any of these risks can result in a loss to the organization because data is not available when needed (see Exhibit 6.2).

Controls to Reduce Risks

There are two areas of risk associated with availability of data. The first is that the technology will be unable to retrieve the needed data in an economical manner, and the second is that the user of that data will not be able to react to business situations on a timely basis.

Both the improper use of technology risk and the inability to react quickly risk can be controlled through the data independence, selection of computer technology, and systems development process strategies. The inability to control technology can be reduced through the accessibility of data, data independence, and competency of people strategies. Note that the major strategy for all of these risks is that of data independence. By using information as a corporate resource, it is more readily available to serve the needs of all users in the organization. When data is "owned" by individual applications, there is a reluctance to make that data available to all interest users. We examine these risks individually.

Reducing the Improper Use of Technology Risk. Many of the problems associated with data processing are attributable to the improper use of technology. The strategies that, if controlled, help reduce this risk are:

1. **Improving Data Independence Strategy Control** Organizations using data base indicate higher skills are needed to effectively use data base technology. Examples of the types of controls that help ensure the proper use of that technology include:
   - *Data Base Administration Procedures* The processes and procedures needed to maintain data independently of applications are developed. The procedures explain how to document data, how to gain access to data, and how data is organized.
   - *Active Data Dictionary* Assurance that the attributes of the data within the data dictionary is enforced by only permitting input and use of that data according to the documented

Exhibit 6.2 Placing Availability Controls Matrix

EDP Risk[a]	Diversity of Data Use	Accessibility of Data	Sharing of Business Systems	Data Independence	Competency of People	Selection of Computer Technology	Systems Development Process	EDP Controls
				Control Strategy				
Improper use of technology	1	2	2	3	2	3	3	1
Inability to react quickly	2	1	2	3	2	3	3	2
Inability to control technology	2	3	2	3	3	2	2	2
Differences[b]								
Human functions replaced with machines						✓	✓	✓
Coded data not readable by people					✓			✓
Rapid processing			✓	✓	✓			✓
Errors preprogrammed	✓				✓	✓	✓	✓
Automation of control		✓	✓	✓		✓	✓	✓
Centralization of functions	✓	✓	✓	✓		✓	✓	✓
New forms of evidence		✓		✓		✓		✓
New methods of authorization		✓		✓	✓	✓		✓
New processing concepts				✓		✓	✓	✓

[a] 3 = high need for control, 2 = average need for control, 1 = low need for control.
[b] ✓ = difference affects control.

attributes. The programming languages accept data definition only from the data dictionary; all other definitions are rejected.

- *Security Officer* An individual responsible for overseeing security for the organization is appointed. This individual has responsibility for administering the data access program and operating the environment security program.

2. **Improving the Selection of Computer Technology Strategy Control** Selection of the technology must be coorindated with the needs of the organization. Examples of controls include:

- *Technology Rating Services* Use of evaluation services such as AUERBACH provide guidance for performance and selection criteria. This service provides independent evaluations, normally obtained from user experience, of hardware and software as guidance to potential users.

- *Vendor Training* Computer technology with associated vendor-supplied manuals and training courses is used. Organizations should incorporate these training opportunities into their data processing training program.

3. **Improving Systems Development Process Strategy Control** The application system should be built to utilize the best technology. The designers need to be familiar with the workings of that technology. Technology should be selected to optimize application processing, rather than having the application modified to fit existing technology. Examples of controls include:

- *Systems and Programmer Training* Training courses on how to use technology effectively are provided. There is no substitute for competent personnel who are adequately trained.

- *Use of Technology Standards* Required ways to use technology are followed. Standards should incorporate the encouragement of good practices and the prevention of bad practices. Standards include methods for systems development, programming, testing, documentation, time reporting, and so forth.

- *Error Analysis* Problems are studied to determine the cause of errors. The conclusions of this study can be used both to correct the error and to prevent the same type of error from recurring.

- *Error Alert* Newsletters to all systems analyst/programmers explain errors that have occurred and how to avoid or correct them. This reduces the recurrence of detected errors.

Reducing the Inability to React Quickly Risk. In today's increasingly competitive business environment, the ability to react to customer needs quickly is important. Communication capabilities, query languages, and data base technology are a few of the technological advances that are helping reduce turnaround time. Controls built into the proper information strategy areas can help ensure adequate information turnaround time. The strategies where controls are most effective in reducing this risk are:

1. **Improving Data Independence Strategy Control** Data base technology splits audit trail information among the data base history logs, data base logs, and application-owned files. Examples of controls that help ensure that users can obtain this information so that they can react quickly include:
   - *Cross-Referenced Audit Trails* Information from one source of data, such as the data base log, is cross-referenced to information in another source of information, such as an application-owned file. Thus the entire audit trail is tied together and easily identified.
   - *Administrative Procedures* Preplanned and detailed procedures and instructions on how to retrieve data reduce the time and effort needed to obtain supporting information.

2. **Improving Selection of Computer Technology Strategy Control** The proper technology, often including special extract languages, is needed to obtain data quickly. Control examples in this area include:
   - *Query Languages* High-level languages designed to retrieve data quickly. These are usually very easy to use languages that help the nondata processing person use computerized data.
   - *Capacity Reports* Monitoring reports indicating communication bottlenecks that delay processing. If computer operations personnel have these reports, they can make the adjustments necessary to improve service.

3. **Improving Systems Development Process Strategy Control** Systems designers need to anticipate future information needs. This preplanning prepares the data environment with the information and processing tools needed. Examples of controls in this area include:
   - *User Involvement in Systems Development* User personnel are assigned to work with the systems development team in specifying and designing computerized applications. This

makes the system the user's system, not data processing's system.

- *Extended Records* These records deliberately attempt to include with history records as much information about processing as practical. This increases the amount of data storage, but also increases the ability to retrieve needed data. It places together all the information relating to an accounting transaction, such as a purchase order, the weekly pay of an employee, and so on.

Reducing the Inability to Control Technology Risk. As much effort must be spent on controlling technology as is spent in determining how it should be used. This is because a major deterrent to the use of technology is the concern on the part of top management that data processing personnel cannot control that technology. Both management and users would be more receptive to using technology if they understood how that technology was to be controlled. The strategies where controls can be placed to lessen this risk include the accessibility of data, data independence, and the competency of people. The controls considered most effective in reducing this risk are:

1. **Improving Accessibility of Data Strategy Control** The key control for relying on data is control over its accessibility. If manage-cannot be assured that accessibility is controlled, it cannot rely on that data. If data can be changed without being detected, there is, in effect, no control over that data. Examples of accessibility controls include:

   - *Accountability* One department, or preferably one individual, is appointed to be accountable for access to each data element. Thus, if problems occur or action is needed, all concerned, including that department or individual, know who is responsible.
   - *Security Profile* A profile describes who can access what data element and for what purposes, such as read only or update. For example, only the credit manager can create, change, or delete a customer's credit limit.
   - *Use of Technology Features* The controls included in the vendor-provided hardware and software are used to control that technology. For example, many communication software systems include passwords as an optional feature, but action must be taken to incorporate those features into the operating environment.

2. **Improving Data Independence Strategy Control** Data base introduces some new control problems associated with the technology. Examples of controls helpful in this area include:

    *   *Data Deadlock Resolution* When two requests block each other from accessing needed data, a method of automatically resolving that deadlock is needed. This data block is sometimes called the deadly embrace.
    *   *Data Base Administrator* A function is established to ensure the effective use of data base technology. The individual is given the responsibility for optimizing the use of data base hardware and software.

3. **Improving Competency of People Strategy Control** There is no substitute for a sufficient supply of adequately trained people. Examples of controls that help ensure this include:

    *   *Training* Provide training sufficient to enable continual maintenance of data processing skills.
    *   *Schedule and Budget Status Reports* Report regularly on the ability of people to meet schedules and budgets. Exceptions may indicate the inability to control technology.
    *   *Acceptance Testing* Involve people who will use the system in debugging systems and changes prior to their use.

PLACING INTEGRITY CONTROLS

Integrity controls ensure the reliability of data. Data is reliable when it has been neither modified nor destroyed, and when the processing that has occurred can be substantiated. High integrity ensures that the computerized information can be relied on in making business decisions.

Need for Integrity Controls

When systems provide reliable data, users are confident that systems reports and decisions made on those reports will be good decisions. When the integrity of information is lost, users often build redundant systems to get reliable data. This occurs frequently and usually proves to be very costly.

Whenever redundant systems must be maintained because of integrity concerns, the value of the primary information system decreases. These redundant systems mean redundant files, extra

Exhibit 6.3 Placing Integrity Control Matrix

	Control Strategy							
	Diversity of Data Use	Accessibility of Data	Sharing of Business Systems	Data Independence	Competency of People	Selection of Computer Technology	Systems Development Process	EDP Controls
EDP Risk[a]								
Concentration of data	1	3	1	3	2	1	2	3
Inability to react quickly	2	1	2	3	2	3	3	2
Inability to substantiate processing	2	1	2	3	1	2	3	3
Inability to control technology	2	3	2	3	3	2	2	2
Concentration of responsibilities	2	3	2	1	2	1	1	3

Differences[b]					
Human functions replaced with machines				✓	✓
Coded data not readable by people			✓		✓
Rapid processing	✓				✓
Errors preprogrammed	✓	✓		✓	✓
Automation of control	✓	✓		✓	✓
Centralization of functions		✓		✓	✓
New forms of evidence		✓			✓
New methods of authorization	✓	✓	✓		✓
New processing concepts		✓		✓	✓

---

[a] 3 = high need for control, 2 = average need for control, 1 = low need for control.
[b] ✓ = difference affects control.

storage of input information, and duplicate processing. Some organizations have built computer systems to check the integrity of other computer systems.

One of the keys to integrity is the ability to reconstruct processing. Even when processing is wrong, if the audit trail substantiates the logic of that processing, people retain faith in the reliability of the systems data. It is normally worth the cost of integrity controls to eliminate unneeded redundancy.

The risks that threaten data integrity include the concentration of data, the inability to react quickly, the inability to substantiate processing, the inability to control technology, and concentration of responsibilities. Placing controls in the appropriate strategies can reduce these risks to an acceptable level (see Exhibit 6.3).

Controls to Reduce Risks

Ensure integrity encompasses all of the information strategies. Addressing controls as part of information strategy can lessen the probability of loss associated with these risks. We examine each risk individually.

Reducing the Concentration of Data Risk. Concentration of data means more dependence on the reliability of a single piece of data. When redundant systems maintain the same data, there is a check between two or more systems. As these redundant systems are eliminated, users become more dependent on a single source of data. Concentrating controls in the availability of data, data independence, and EDP controls strategies helps lessen the probability of loss due to these risks.

1. **Improving Accessibility of Data Strategy Control** If data is readily accessible, opportunity to lose data integrity increases. Examples of controls effective in this strategy include:
   - *Limit Hours of Accessibility* Users can access data only during normal business hours. Control is normally strongest during working hours, and that is also the normal time for access.
   - *Limit Terminals* Place a restriction on which terminals can access all or parts of the data. This is a means of segregating functions.

2. **Improving Data Independence Strategy Control** Maintaining data independently of the programs shifts much of the control over integrity from application systems to the environment. A control example is the *data base verification programs*, which are utility programs designed to verify the integrity of data. They examine the data in the data base to verify that all that is supposed to be there is, in fact, there.

3. **Improving EDP Control Strategy Control.** EDP controls should provide independent assurance that the integrity of data is ensured. Examples of controls in this area include:

   - *User-Maintained Control Totals* User department procedures independently verify its data base elements. The users maintain duplicate control totals.
   - *Password Change Procedures* Procedures are developed to change passwords on a regular basis and when people leave or a password is compromised.

Reducing the Inability to React Quickly Risk. An important aspect of integrity is being able to provide answers to problems quickly. Even if data is correct, people must be able to verify that correctness within a reasonable period or else customers of the system may lose confidence in the data. The areas where controls can be most effective are in the data independence, selection of computer technology, and systems development process strategies.

1. **Improving Data Independence Strategy Control** Having data independent of programs does not guarantee ready accessibility. This happens only with sufficient advance planning. Examples of controls in this area include:

   - *Query Languages* Flexible high-level extract languages are used.
   - *Before and After Images* There is ready access to data not currently maintained in a data base. Logs can be maintained that show the status of data both before and after processing.

2. **Improving Selection of Computer Technology Strategy Control** Hardware and software must be in type and quantity sufficient to enable data to be retrieved quickly. Controls include *capacity monitoring*, which determines that sufficient capacity exists for users to obtain data when needed.

3. **Improving Systems Development Process Strategy Control**   The user's desires must be anticipated in the systems development process. Controls here include *structured design*, a systematic development process that makes modification with minimal effort. The process shows in detail how output reports are developed, thus documenting all the places affected by a change.

Reducing the Inability to Substantiate Processing Risk.   Closely allied to getting data quickly is verifying the current status of that data. This includes a complete trail that shows step by step how the current values were derived. Controls in three strategies help lessen this risk. The strategies of data independence, systems development process, and EDP controls are the desirable areas for control.

1. **Improving Data Independence Strategy Control**   Independent data requires independent audit trails. Controls here include:
   - *Before and After Images*   These images provide the evidence to verify what occurred during processing, and shows the value before and after a particular processing event occurred.
   - *Audit Trail Documentation*   This explains the trail from data origination through control totals and is an application-specified audit trail, requiring the same planning as all other aspects of systems processing.

2. **Improving Systems Development Process Strategy Control**   The audit trail development must be an integral part of the development process. Controls here include an *internal audit systems development review*, which is an independent analysis of the inadequacy of the audit trail. The internal auditors should be asked to determine whether the proposed audit trail is adequate and complies with governmental requirements.

3. **Improving EDP Controls Strategy Control**   Conformance to regulations is an important part of substantiating processing. Controls include:
   - *Internal Revenue Service Requirements Checklist*   A checklist should be used to verify conformance to Internal Revenue Service Procedure 64-12 and Ruling 71-20. The U.S. procedures apply to the use and retention of computer data for tax purposes.
   - *Foreign Corrupt Practices Act Checklist*   A checklist should be used to verify conformance to the requirements of the act. This process determines whether an organization's controls

are adequate to meet the internal control requirements of the act.

Reducing the Inability to Control Technology Risk. The integrity of data can be lost because of problems in the hardware and software. Controls must determine that these problems are either prevented or detected. The strategies where controls are most effective are accessibility to data, data independence, and competency of people.

1. **Improving Accessibility to Data Strategy Control** Controls in the hardware should protect data from everyday mistakes, inadvertent erroneous processing, and the like. Controls include:
    *   *Memory Protect Features* These hardware or software features prevent data from being modified by programs outside the protected area. This prevents one area of processing in computer storage from accessing another area of processing.
    *   *Automatic Shutdown* Hardware features stop processing when problems are detected. For example, if someone enters an invalid password several times, processing from that terminal can be stopped.
2. **Improving Data Independence Strategy Control** Centralized data bases utilize new and complex technology that is undergoing rapid changes. Problems can cause data to be lost. Controls include:
    *   *Broken Pointer Search* Utility programs verify the accuracy and completeness of pointers. If a pointer is broken (i.e., a chain is broken), data can be lost.
    *   *Overnight Batch Processing* Data is processed by on-line methods during the day and is then reprocessed overnight using batch processing. The results of the two processing methods are then compared to ensure accuracy of the on-line processing.
3. **Improving Competency of People Strategy Control** Well-trained people can anticipate and prepare for technological problems. Controls include:
    *   *Updating Services* Subscribe to services that regularly publish technological problems. This provides an independent appraisal of vendor-produced hardware and software.
    *   *User Groups* Become active in user groups, which include organizations using the same technology and in the same

industry, to keep abreast of current technological problems and of how other organizations use technology and solve technological problems.

Reducing the Concentration of Responsibilities Risks. A major threat to integrity is people. Without the proper checks and balances, people can circumvent controls. Controls should be included in the accessibility of data and EDP control strategies.

1. **Improving Accessibility of Data Strategy Control** People should be restricted in their accessibility to data. Controls include:
   - *Restricted Entry to Computer Room* Only authorized people are permitted in the computer room.
   - *Restricted Systems Commands* Limit the use of system commands to people who are specifically authorized to use them.
   - *Complete Security Profile* All individuals enabled to use computer resources have a systems defined and enforced security profile. This profile is then used to enforce access and processing restrictions.

2. **Improving EDP Controls Strategy Control** Administrative controls should be imposed on individuals in positions of responsibility. These types of controls include:
   - *Review Accounts of Key Personnel* People in positions of authority who have a company account, such as payroll, tax deposits, savings accounts, and so on, should have those accounts reviewed periodically by auditors or management.
   - *Loyalty Oaths* Individuals are asked to sign statements indicating loyalty to their organization. This is helpful in showing management's intent.

PLACING RECOVERY CONTROLS

In a computerized business environment, recovery takes on more importance. Knowledge is not resident with people but, rather, with computerized systems. There are three aspects of recovery, which are backup, restart, and recovery. Backup is the collection of data for restart and recovery purposes. Restart is beginning the system after it has stopped. Recovery is restarting the system after a problem has occurred. The risks lessening recovery capabilities are improper use of technology, inability to substantiate processing, and inability to control technology.

Need for Recovery Controls

Organizations become dependent on information provided by computerized applications. Should this information be lost, so might many business transactions. For example, if the customer accounts receivable file were lost, the company might lose many of those receivable balances. One large corporation nearly went bankrupt when it lost its accounts receivable file. Recovery provides management assurance that data and processing will not be lost in the event of problems (see Exhibit 6.4).

Controls to Reduce Risks

Recovery controls are an important aspect of data processing. Many of the problems associated with data processing are attributable to the inability to recovery computer information after systems problems. For example, service levels may be reduced while the computer department determines how to recover.

In the data base technology, recovery takes on even greater importance. This is because more data is concentrated in one area, and the loss of that data would have an impact on the organization greater than when data was split among many files. Also, there are multiple users processing and using that data concurrently.

Having multiple users of data makes both restart and recovery more difficult after problems have been encountered. We will examine each of these risks individually to illustrate the controls effective in reducing these risks.

Reducing the Improper Use of Technology Risk. Computer technology is needed to recover from computer problems. The intricacies of computer processing are too complex for people to go through all the steps needed for recovery. Therefore, many of them are automated. The controls over technology are most effective when incorporated into data independence, selection of computer technology, and systems development process strategies.

1. **Improving Data Independence Strategy Control** When data is maintained independently of programs, the recovery for that data must also be independent of the application programs. Controls include:
   - *Restart Utilities* Utility programs designed to restart a data

Exhibit 6.4 Placing Recovery Controls Matrix

	Control Strategy							
	Diversity of Data Use	Accessibility of Data	Sharing of Business Systems	Data Independence	Competency of People	Selection of Computer Technology	Systems Development Process	EDP Controls
EDP Risk[a]								
Improper use of technology	1	2	2	3	2	3	3	1
Inability to substantiate processing	2	1	2	3	1	2	3	3
Inability to control technology	2	3	2	3	3	2	2	2
Differences[b]								
Replace people functions with machines						✓	✓	✓

Coded data not readable by people

Rapid processing

Errors preprogrammed

Automation of control

Centralization of functions

New forms of evidence

New methods of authorization

New processing concepts

---

[a] 3 = high need for control, 2 = average need for control, 1 = low need for control.
[b] √ = difference affects control.

base operation automate a process that is very difficult to perform under manual control.

- *Recovery Utilities* Utility programs are designed to back up a data base system to the point of the problem and restart processing at that point to recovery operation.

2. **Improving Selection of Computer Technology Strategy Control** Sufficient hardware must be available to aid the recovery process. Part of the technology is needed for backup, and the remainder is needed for recovery purposes. Controls include:

- *Duplicate Hardware* Alternate hardware that can assume processing should the first system go down may be useful, but doubles the cost unless there is additional work for the alternate hardware.
- *Excess Data Capacity* Extra capacity for data storage is valuable to improve performance and hold extra data if the need occurs.

3. **Improving Systems Development Process Strategy Control** The systems development process must compensate for recovery weaknesses in the data base and other nonapplication parts of the system. Controls not included in the environment must be included in the application. Environmental controls include *restart procedures*, which are standardized methods of stopping and starting systems in the event of problems. This standardized method helps eliminate mistakes during the restart process.

Reducing the Inability to Substantiate Processing Risk. Completeness of data is aided with adequate recovery of data procedures. Recovery includes reconstruction after a processing problem. The recovery process must be able to back up to some past time and reconstruct processing without user involvement. Recovery controls are best placed in the data independence, systems development process, and EDP controls strategies.

1. **Improving Data Independence Strategy Control** Processing in the data base must be substantiated through data base recovery controls. These controls include:

- *Before and After Image Log* The log shows the status of data before and after processing and is used as the basis for processing from the point where integrity of the data base has been ensured.
- *Backup Copies* Regularly making a backup copy of the en-

tire data base establishes a point of ensured integrity of the data base.

2. **Improving Systems Development Process Strategy Control** The nondata base processing segment is responsible for substantiating the application processing. This includes history tapes and audit trails of processing. Controls include:

- *System Checkpoints* The integrity of the system is recorded at selected times. It is at these points that backup data is obtained for the purpose of recovery should problems occur.
- *Record Retention Program* Saving inputs, history logs, and other parts of the system until no longer needed satisfies organizational and legal requirements.

3. **Improving EDP Controls Strategy Control** Procedures should be established to ensure that the other strategies adequately safeguard the system. Controls include:

- *Time and Date Stamps* Indicating in a transaction the time and date of origination or processing allows the sequence of processing to be restructured.
- *Recovery Documentation* This provides a detailed description of the data saved and the procedures needed to recover the operation in the event problems occur.
- *Record Retention Policy* The policy to save data for recovery and other purposes is formalized, stating what will be saved and for how long.

Reducing the Inability to Control Technology Risk. Recovery has proven one of the more difficult tasks in an on-line data base environment. Most of the serious data base problems have been associated with recovery. The strategies where controls should be placed to lessen this risk include accessibility of data, data independence, and competency of people.

1. **Improving Accessibility of Data Strategy Control** Large numbers of multiple users, coupled with the centralization of data, tax technologies' capabilities to handle all aspects of recovery. Controls that have proven effective include *disaster tests*, which stimulate unusual processing to test the adequacy of controls. These tests, by simulating a disaster and asking operations personnel to recover, determine whether recovery procedures work.

2. **Improving Data Independence Strategy Control** Using data base changes the methods by which processing occurs. Data can be

entered into the data base without performing normal processing. In other words, the data is stored in the data base until the appropriate processing time. Technology must control into which accounting period data belongs. Controls include *dating transactions*, or putting a date and/or time in a transaction so that its appropriate accounting periods can be readily identified. This procedure helps record transactions in the appropriate accounting period.

3. **Improving Competency of People Strategy Controls**   Part of the problem of recovery is that it is not a regular occurrence. Because it is so seldom used, it is subject to error. Controls to lessen these problems include:

    *   *Recovery Drills*   Computer operators practice recovery procedures. This prepares the operators to recover in the event a real problem occurs.
    *   *Documented Recovery Procedures*   Detailed step-by-step procedures are written that describe how to recover computer operations after a problem.

SUMMARY

In a computerized business environment, controls over that environment help ensure its success. As functions such as data base and communications become centralized, more reliance must be placed on environmental controls. This is a shift in emphasis in both the design and operation of computerized business applications.

In a noncomputerized environment, these environmental controls are normally procedures. As sytems become computerized so do some of the environmental controls. However, these lag in automation behind application controls. With the newer technologies, more and more controls are becoming automated in the environmental area. Both the approach to controls and the approach to systems design are changing, because the functions being automated are being moved from the application area and automated in the environmental area.

CHAPTER **7**

Controlling the Integrity of Data

Users of data processing systems have both primary and shared control responsibilities. Those controls that affect all applications, such as security, are control responsibilities shared by all users of the data processing resources. Each user has the primary responsibilities for control over his or her own area of authority. For example, the payroll manager has responsibility for the preparation of an accurate and complete payroll.

Controls that are the primary responsibility of a single user are normally called application controls. As data processing applications move to on-line data base environments, many of the application control responsibilities move to the environment. Even with this movement, there are many control responsibilities that remain with the user. The data processing systems analyst/programmer should work with the users to design and implement controls.

Those functions not covered by the environment remain individual user control responsibilities. Part of the application control responsibilities include determining that the environmental controls are adequate and functioning properly. Some of this responsibility is shared with other users, but in some cases a user will want to build applica-

131

tion controls that verify the proper functioning of environmental controls. This is particularly true in the data base environment where multiple users are using the same data, but one user should still be accountable for that data.

AREAS OF APPLICATION CONTROL RESPONSIBILITY

Computerized applications are designed to process data. Most computerized applications are designed to satisfy specific needs. The systems analysis function and programming result in building a one-of-a-kind system. This is costly and has resulted in a trend toward generalized applications. Part of this trend is attributable to the many small organizations getting computers. They cannot afford the luxury of designing and writing a special-purpose application, whereas a generalized application can often be economically modified to meet any needs.

In the United States it is estimated that there are 50,000 different payroll applications. Knowing that it is difficult to calculate pay 50,000 different ways, we can assume there must be a large amount of redundancy in these payroll systems. For this reason, many small organizations opt to use the generalized packages, which are normally more structured than specially built systems.

Most computerized applications follow a structured processing path (see Figure 7.1). This path starts with a need to be satisfied that is converted into an input transaction for a computerized application. The input is then processed using data in storage. Output is prepared for use by the person or group originating the need.

On-line data base processing involves the same steps, but not necessarily in the same sequence. A data base environment implies data is retained in one central storage area. With on-line processing, the data can be put into storage as soon as practical. This enables users to place that data in storage and hold it until the appropriate time for processing. For example, if customer A wanted product B delivered in two weeks, that order could be put into the data base. It could be held there for two weeks and then processed automatically at the appropriate time. In data base systems, processing often follows a sequence different from that of nondata base systems, but the same basic steps are still executed (i.e., input, process, storage, and output).

The owner of the application is responsible for the accuracy, completeness, and authorization of data as it is processed through the

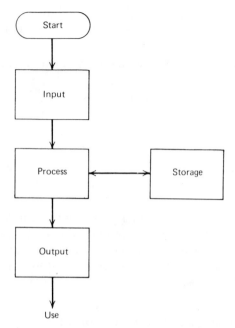

Figure 7.1 **Application System Functions.**

various steps of the application system. Application controls should be designed to ensure the accuracy, completeness, and authorization of data while under the control of the application. In addition, the users of the application should be held responsible for controls that ensure the integrity and consistency of data as it is used by others.

Scope of Application Controls

Application control commences when data is originated for computerized applications. Ideally, control should commence when the transaction is initiated, but that is not always practical. For example, customers preparing orders may send them through the mail to the company that will fulfill that order. Although it would be nice to know that customer X as just completed and dropped an order in the mailbox, it is not practical to begin control until the data is received by the fulfilling company. Once that data is prepared for the computerized application, it should be controlled.

For the purposes of explaining and designing application controls, controls are divided into the following functions:

- *Input* Data is originated and transcribed into a machine-readable format, and that data is entered into a terminal or other input device.
- *Process* Data is processed while under the control of the application programs.
- *Storage* Data is retained and controlled in dedicated files and/or a centralized data base.
- *Output* Data is converted from storage to a form readable by users, output includes delivery of that information to the user.
- *Use* The desired result of the application, such as making a decision based on computer-produced data, is obtained.

The user must determine which of these five functions is the most cost-effective area for placing control. Some risks should be controlled during input, whereas other risks are more appropriately controlled in other areas of the application system. Also, the type of control used affects costs.

Preventive, Detective, and Corrective Controls

Application controls can be preventive, detective, or corrective. Preventive controls stop an event from occurring, detective controls disclose that a problem has occurred, and corrective controls provide the data necessary to correct errors that have been detected.

These three types of controls can be illustrated in a fire protection system. Designing a fireproof computer room is a preventive control to stop fire from occurring. However, should it occur, a fire alarm is a detective control that alerts people to the fact that a fire has occurred. Fire extinguishers are corrective controls that can be used to put out the fire once it has been detected. These three types of controls are used in application systems.

The type of control selected involves two considerations: first, whether the transaction should be stopped prior to the start of processing; and second, where the most cost-effective place to put the controls is.

We would think that all controls would be of the preventive type, but preventive controls are not always practical or possible. For example, it would be difficult to prevent customers who have exceeded their credit limits from placing orders. The objective of control is to stop these customers from receiving any more goods. If a preventive control was established, the application would have to reject each order at the point where the customer placed the order. This would require some special extensive controls at each order entry point, which would involve determining the cost of the new order. If a detective control is used, the order can be entered like any other order and processed until the appropriate customer credit information could be obtained. This will probably be during the processing step of the application, when the order is normally priced. At that point, the credit overrun would be detected, and the order would be stopped. The net effect is the same as if a listing of customer numbers with unused credit was given to each order entry clerk to prevent the order from being accepted at its point of entry. Detective controls should be selected when they are the most cost-effective to use.

In other situations, the transaction must be prevented from entering the system. This might occur when someone who wants access to a specific record gains access to it; all that a detective control can do is state that the compromise has been made. It may be too late to stop the loss, so in that case a preventive control is warranted. Where the risks occur can be illustrated using a matrix.

EDP Risks/Systems Function Matrix

The objective of control in applications is to reduce the probability of loss due to risks. Some of the risks that are unique to or increased in a computerized business environment should not be controlled in the computerized application, because the risks apply to all applications and should therefore be reduced with environmental controls. However, if there are no environmental controls over those risks, then each application must build its own controls.

An example of a risk common to all applications is the improper use of technology. The proper use of technology should be achieved through selecting hardware and software, hiring and training competent computer people, developing standards, and so on. But certain types of risks, such as the cascading of errors, cannot be controlled at the environmental level and are best controlled at the application level.

Where to place controls is normally a cost-effectiveness decision. If it is more effective to place the control at the environmental level, that is where it should be placed. When it is more effective to control at the application level, control should be placed there.

The interrelationship between EDP risks and the five systems functions is illustrated in Exhibit 7.1. This matrix shows where there is a

Exhibit 7.1 EDP Risks/Systems Function Matrix

	Systems Function				
	Input	Process	Storage	Output	Use
EDP Risk[a]					
Cascading of errors	2	3	1	1	3
Illogical processing	2	3	1	2	3
Inability to translate needs into technical requirements	2	3	2	3	1
Inability to control technology	2	3	2	2	3
Repetition of errors	2	3	1	2	3
Concentration of responsibilities	1	1	3	1	3
Incorrect entry of data	3	3	1	2	3

[a]3 = high need for control, 2 = average need for control, 1 = low need for control.

high need for control, an average need for control, and a low need for control. For example, the cascading of errors risk is shown as best controlled in the process and use functions of an application system, as this is where there is a high need for control.

The controls should be placed in those functions where the risk is greatest or, in other words, where the need for control is highest. Systems designers can use this matrix to help them select the points in an application where controls are normally most cost-effective.

Application Control Objectives

An application control is placed in one of the five application functions to reduce a risk. It is difficult to place a control to achieve a specific control objective without knowing the risk. To explain this, let's examine the completeness of data control objective. In a manual system, we could assign someone the task of determining that data is complete. Although this is difficult to achieve, the individual could achieve part of the objective by continually looking for unentered transactions or by asking all involved parties which transactions had not been entered. This is not practical in a computerized application. Application controls are located in specific functions. Let's look at what can be done to verify completeness. In the input function, we can include a record count as a control to help ensure completeness. In addition, we can develop a batch total that can be checked during the process function to help ensure completeness, and we can put out a special report so that in the use function the user can verify that complete processing has occurred. To do this properly, however, it helps to know where the risks affecting completeness are located so appropriate controls can be implemented.

Applications are responsible for determining that data is complete, accurate, authorized, and consistent. Controls should be established in the application to achieve these four control objectives. The following sections examine these four objectives individually.

PLACING COMPLETENESS CONTROLS

The objective of completeness is to ensure that all transactions entering the system are processed and available for output when needed. Completeness involves every function in the application system. It is one of the basic control objectives in data processing. The risk of loss of data, and thus incomplete processing, is always present.

Need for Completeness Controls

Completeness controls help ensure the ongoing success of an organization. Organizations cannot continually lose large amounts of data and maintain a viable organization. The loss of assets and customer confidence would soon put that organization out of business.

Among the reasons for incomplete processing are:

- *Loss of Input Data* Data is mislaid, misdirected, or destroyed prior to its entry into the computerized application.
- *Overlay* One record is laid over the top of another and thus lost.
- *Program Error* The program fails to process a record. In a tape batch system this sometimes happens to the last record on the file.
- *Loss during System Shutdown* If the system encounters a failure, data in queues or in communication facilities can be lost.
- *Loss of Output Data* Individual transactions or records, such as invoices, purchase orders, and the like, may never reach the designated location.

- *Hardware or Software Failure*   A problem in hardware or vendor-produced software can cause a record to be lost.

Controls should attempt to prevent these types of losses from occurring, but, if they occur, controls should detect that loss. In addition, there should be sufficient controls to correct the problem once it has been detected.

Controls to Reduce Risks

There are four risks that threaten completeness of processing. These are illogical processing, inability to translate needs into technical requirements, inability to control technology, and repetition of errors. Controls should be incorporated into the various sytems functions to lessen the probability of loss associated with these risks (see Exhibit 7.2). Note that the matrix shows the differences between a manual and a computerized environment that need to be addressed by these controls.

Reducing the Illogical Processing Risk.   Computer systems follow a preestablished pattern. This pattern normally involves obtaining a record, processing it, and then getting another record. If errors in processing (i.e., illogical processing) cause a deviation from this pattern, records can be lost.

The two functions most appropriate to reduce the illogical processing risk are the process and use functions. Illogical processing can be prevented in the process function and detected in the use function. Sufficient corrective controls must be incorporated into the process function so that if an error is detected it can be corrected.

1. **Improving Process Control**   Illogical processing that threatens to lose data needs to be controlled in the process function. Controls here serve two preventive purposes: to prevent losing data or records and to prevent destruction of needed data. The controls that are effective include:
    - *Program Testing*   Preparing test data to verify that all data is processed should test the controls over read and write of actions in each program.
    - *Input Record Counts*   Manually or automatically count the records during input and then continually verify that all the records have been received and processed.

Exhibit 7.2   Placing Completeness Controls Matrix

	Systems Function				
	Input	Process	Storage	Output	Use
EDP Risk[a]					
Illogical processing	2	3	1	2	3
Inability to translate needs into technical requirements	2	3	2	3	1
Inability to control technology	2	3	2	2	3
Repetition of errors	2	3	1	2	3
Differences[b]					
Human functions replaced with machines	✓	✓			
Coded data not readable by people	✓			✓	✓
Rapid processing		✓		✓	✓
Errors preprogrammed		✓		✓	✓
Automation of control	✓	✓	✓	✓	
Centralization of functions			✓		✓
New forms of evidence	✓		✓	✓	✓
New methods of authorization	✓				✓
New processing concepts	✓	✓	✓	✓	✓

[a] 3 = high need for control, 2 = average need for control, 1 = low need for control.
[b] ✓ = difference affects control.

2. **Improving Use Control**   The user has a responsibility to verify the completeness of processing. This can be done by maintaining controls independently of the computerized application or by using information obtained from the application. Controls here include:

- *External Record Counts*   Maintain counts of inputted transactions and verify that they have all been processed. For example, the counts may determine that one payroll check has been produced for each employee. This is normally done by users.

- *User Complaints* Verify the cause of reported loss of data. One of the best sources to identify problems is users inquiring about lack of service.

Reducing the Inability to Translate Needs into Technical Requirements Risk. Users need to specify the types and quantities of data going into computerized applications. Failure to communicate this information can result in the loss of data going into computerized applications. Usually this loss is associated with unusual transactions. For example, last-minute adjustments to payroll may not be entered.

Controls over the inability to translate needs into technical requirements should be built into the process and output functions of a system. The process segment should detect missing transactions. The output function should provide an audit trail sufficient to show users of the report whether all transactions are included.

1. **Improving Process Control** Systems analysts should attempt to anticipate potential completeness problems and build controls into the process segment of the application to look for problems. These types of detective controls include *anticipation messages*, which are warning messages designed to alert user personnel to the possibility of missing data. For example, if a batch of input is overdue, a message should be put out alerting people to a potential problem.

2. **Improving Output Control** Included in the output report should be information sufficient to enable user to detect missing data. The type of information could include number of transactions, dollar amount of transactions, dates of transactions, and so on. Controls of this type include:

   - *Report Totals* Totals are organized by various categories for the purpose or verifying completeness of data. Users should be able to verify these totals against independent totals to determine whether data is missing.
   - *Counts* Total number of departments, people, units, and so forth, are included in the report. Again, these counts are verified to independently maintained counts.

Reducing the Inability to Control Technology Risk. Computer technology poses threats to completeness. Loss can occur due to either a hardware or software malfunction. This is particularly true in an on-line data base technology. Large amounts of data move over communication lines and are stored in a centralized data base.

Without sufficient controls, data could be lost and not readily detected.

The inability to control technology risk can best be controlled in the process and use functions of a system. The process function is used to prevent problems, whereas the use function is used to detect problems.

1. **Improving Process Control**   Controls over technology in processing should verify the movement of data through the hardware and software. The movement can be from terminal to computer, from computer to terminal, or within the data base. These controls verify that all data entered or written can be retrieved when desired. Controls include:

   - *Header Labels* A record indicates the type of information on a file. This is normally the first record on the file, and its purpose is to describe both the contents and date of the file.
   - *Trailer Labels* A record in a file indicates the number of records or other totals within the file. This is normally the last record on a file, and its purpose is to contain control total information.
   - *Sequence Numbers* Sequentially increasing numbers are given to transactions to account for all records entered. A processing routine verifies that all numbers are accounted for during processing.

2. **Improving Use Control**   User controls place the burden on the user to detect technological problems. To do this, the user must have a good understanding of the computer data and the control over the data. The major advantage the user has over data processing personnel in detecting problems is an intimate knowledge of the data. User controls over technological problems include:

   - *External Control Totals* Control information is maintained independently of the computer application to verify completeness of computer processing.
   - *Scanning* Someone familiar with the data reviews output to verify the reasonableness of the data in the report.

Reducing the Repetition of Errors Risk. Problems that occur in data processing are normally repeated for all like conditions. For example, if a record of type X is excluded from processing, all records of type X will be excluded from processing. This magnifies the impact of an error many times over. Therefore, when a particular completeness error has been uncovered, additional investigation must be undertaken to determine that all errors of that type have been caught.

Controls to reduce the risk of repetition of errors should be located in the process and use functions of an application system. The process function attempts to prevent the repetition of errors through elimination of problems. The use function enables the user to detect this type of problem.

1. **Improving Process Control** The best method for avoiding repetition of errors is to avoid the initial error. This can be accomplished by good systems design, adequate testing, and sufficient audits of input data. Controls include an *automatic batch check*, in which the control totals either entered or accumulated at the beginning of processing are verified against the totals at the end of processing.

2. **Improving Use Control** The repetition of errors is normally easier to locate then the cascading of errors. For example, if one or more print positions is broken, normally this is readily apparent to the eye. If the type of error is extensive, such as printing every payroll check for $1 million too much, that, too, is easily detected. But more subtle errors that are repeated can be difficult to detect. Repetition of error controls include, aside from *scanning* (just defined), *change of condition warning messages*. If prices are changed or some other aspect of programs has changed, this type of information should be sent to the people who scan the output so that they can look for problems associated with that changing condition.

PLACING ACCURACY CONTROLS

Accuracy governs the content of a transaction as opposed to its inclusion or deletion. Accuracy means both that the data is entered correctly and that it is entered in accordance with the organization's policies and procedures. The policies and procedures should be consistent with current laws and regulations.

The accuracy of data is affected by the recording and processing of data. The threats to accuracy from these causes include:

- Misinterpretation of the data by a data entry clerk.
- Entering the wrong data by the originator.

- Transposing digits or letters.
- Entering data in the wrong position or part of a form.
- Program error.
- Hardware or vendor-supplied software error.
- Processing against the wrong account (e.g., using the wrong price for a product).
- Failure to follow an organizational policy and procedure (e.g., giving a customer a discount on a payment after the 30-day discount period expires).

Accuracy also includes adherence to regulations and laws. Problems in this area include:

- Inadequate cost-effective controls.
- Recording data in the wrong accounting period.
- Failure to safeguard private information.
- Failure to disclose the proper intent of a transaction.
- Violation of a law (e.g., paying under the minimum wage).

The risks that result in inaccurate data include the cascading of errors, illogical processing, inability to translate needs into technical requirements, inability to control technology, and repetition of errors.

Need for Accuracy Controls

Inaccuracy is a continual threat to an organization. The largest category of loss attributable to data processing has been called "errors and omissions." Omissions result in incomplete processing, whereas errors result in inaccurate processing. Most errors are caused by carelessness on the part of employees or lack of adequate supervision. Controls help lessen the probability of loss due to risks (see Exhibit 7.3).

Controls to Reduce Risks

One of the more prevalent areas of control is that ensuring accurate processing. Many of the inaccuracies are caused by the problem unique to or increased in computerized applications. Therefore,

Exhibit 7.3   Placing Accurate Controls Matrix

	Systems Function				
	Input	Process	Storage	Output	Use
EDP Risk[a]					
Cascading of errors	2	3	1	1	3
Illogical processing	2	3	1	2	3
Inability to translate needs into technical requirements	2	3	2	3	1
Inability to control technology	2	3	2	2	3
Repetition of errors	2	3	1	2	3
Differences[b]					
Human functions replaced with machines	√	√			
Coded data not readable by people	√			√	√
Rapid processing		√		√	√
Errors preprogrammed		√		√	√
Automation of control	√	√	√	√	
Centralization of functions			√		√
New forms of evidence	√		√	√	√
New methods of authorization	√				√
New processing concepts	√	√	√	√	√

[a] 3 = high need for control, 2 = average need for control, 1 = low need for control.
[b] √ = difference affects control.

when designing accuracy controls, special attention should be placed on the differences.

Reducing the Cascading of Errors Risk.   Cascading of errors is a risk unique to data processing. It is a chain reaction of inaccurate processing. The reaction is triggered by an unusual condition that then cascades through the automated processing of the system, creating more and more errors in later programs.

The cascading of errors is the type of event that one hopes to prevent. The better designed and tested systems tend to have fewer errors of this type. Preventive controls can be placed in the process function of a system; detective controls should be placed in the user area.

1. **Improving Process Control**   The process function should be built so that the relationship between systems has been adequately designed. This type of risk is an interprogram or intersystem condition. Controls include:

   - *Structured Systems Design*   This orderly process shows the interrelationship of design among all functions of a system and is a design methodology that shows the data relationship between programs, the data base, source of data, and reports.
   - *Prompting*   A terminal user is led through the terminal process so that he or she becomes familiar enough with it to avoid errors. This control uses a series of questions and tips to help a terminal operator process a transaction correctly.

2. **Improving Use Control**   The cascading of inaccuracies frequently results in a large number of concurrent problems. When this happens, one should suspect the cascading of errors risk. Controls include *scanning* (defined earlier) and a *control clerk*, who is an individual appointed to oversee the accuracy and completeness of processing from one or more applications. This individual may work either for data processing or the user.

Reducing the Illogical Processing Risk.   Illogical processing is another risk unique to data processing. It is the type of processing that should not happen but does, for example, automatically reordering large amounts of a product that is not selling.

As with most accuracy and completeness risks, preventive controls are installed in the process function of a system and detective controls in the use function.

1. **Improving Process Control**   Illogical processing can occur when untested paths of a computer program are executed. It can also occur when a combination of paths are executed for the first time, such as ordering two products for the first time in a single order. Controls include:

   - *Error Testing*   Use bad data to test system error routines. The more conditions that are tested, the less likely that an error will occur during production.

- *Mapping* This automated procedure isolates unused segments of a computer program. This control looks for segments of computer code that are not used, which then should be investigated, as they may not have been tested.

2. **Improving Use Controls** In most instances, illogical processing results in an error that is obvious to a control-oriented person. However, some controls can be automated to detect many of these errors. Controls include *scanning* (defined earlier) and *output audits*, which check the reasonableness of and limits on output information; for example, the size of a payroll check for clerical people might be limited to $500 per week.

Reducing the Inability to Translate Needs into Technical Requirements Risk. The appearance of this risk in all the application areas is indicative of how great a threat is posed by this risk. Most of the inaccuracies could be avoided with complete systems specification. This requires an in-depth dialogue between the user and the analyst describing as many processing conditions as practical, together with the results desired from those conditions.

Controls to ensure that specifications are sufficient should be built into the process and output functions of a system. These controls are normally designed by data processing personnel to account for conditions that have not been adequately specified. Many of these are the "can't possibly happen" conditions, but these conditions need to be provided for in the application.

1. **Improving Process Control** The process function must compensate for the lack of specifications. The system cannot contain open processing loops. For example, if three codes are permitted, a fourth condition must be included to handle all other codes—those that can't possibly occur, but do. Controls include:
   - *Catch-All Processing* These routines are designed to process any code or condition that occurs, even if that processing is to reject the transaction.
   - *Default Option* Uncertain conditions are translated into the most logical conditions and users are notified to verify the action. If no order date is included, for example, the default option might be to insert today's date.
2. **Improving Output Control** The information leaving the system should be subjected to the same rigorous audits as input. Thus many of the unspecified conditions would be caught. For exam-

ple, if a payroll system only allowed 99.9 hours of work per pay period, when an employee reached 100 hours the result would be zero hours of pay. An output audit looking for net pay of less than $10 might catch this type of error. Controls include *output audits*, which check reasonableness of and limits on output information, limiting, for example, the size of a payroll check for clerical people to between $10 and $500 per week.

Reducing the Inability to Control Technology Risk. Automated processing is prone to inaccuracies. Hardware and software vendors build many redundancies into their product to help improve accuracy. Systems analysts should analyze those redundancies to determine areas of potential porblems. For example, if the hardware circuitry performs mathematical functions twice and compares results, there is little need for the systems analyst to repeat that process. But if the system relies on the accuracy of a single field, the systems designer may wish to add a check digit to ensure the accuracy of that field.

Controls over this risk should be installed in the process function to prevent technological problems and in the use function to detect them should they occur.

1. **Improving Process Control**   Systems analysts should incorporate controls to verify the accuracy of the technology. These should be designed to complement the controls provided by the hardware and software vendors. Controls include:
   - *Check Digit*   A character added to the end of a field or record checks both the accuracy and positioning of the numbers of a field or record. The data is accumulated by a mathematical formula and then checked to a check digit that is the correct answer.
   - *Hash Totals*   Adding alphanumeric information to accumulate a meaningless total verifies the accuracy of data within one or more fields. For example, names are added to arrive at a control total, verifying that all the names are in the file correctly.

2. **Improving Use Controls**   People should monitor the technology that they use. The user is in the best position to monitor technology, because the user is familiar with the data. Controls include:
   - *Data Playback*   The entered information is displayed back to

the individual entering the data so it can be visually verified. The playback often uses a variation of the entered data. For example, if a clerk enters part number, the playback is part name.

- *Process Confirmation*   After processing has occurred, the user is sent data that verifies transaction processing. After depositing funds in the bank, for example, a user would be given a slip showing the old balance, the deposit, and the new balance.

Reducing the Repetition of Errors Risk.   The consistency of data processing applies equally to inaccuracies. If the computer incorrectly processes a transaction of a specific type, all transactions of that type will be incorrectly processed. Therefore, whenever an inaccuracy occurs in a computerized application, it must be determined whether that error has been repeated in all the transactions of that type.

The repetition of errors can be disastrous for EDP departments if it is not detected quickly. Controls should be established in the process and use functions to help detect problems of this type.

1. **Improving Process Control**   The process function should anticipate the repetition of errors. Controls include a *control alert*, which documents and circulates the occurrence of an error so that all involved parties are aware the problem has occurred and can check their work to determine if it, too, has been subject to that error.

2. **Improving Use Control**   The repetition of errors problem should be continually addressed by users. Once an error is detected, the question should be asked if there are more just like it. Controls include an *error search*, during which all events or transactions of a specific type for which an error has been detected are examined to determine whether errors have been repeated.

PLACING CONSISTENCY CONTROLS

In addition to being complete and accurate, data must be consistent. One of the basic concepts of accounting is the consistency of data from accounting period to accounting period. This enables people to make logical comparisons. For example, if the profit of a company was $1 for the last period and $2 for this period, we could assume that profits had doubled. However, this assumes that data has been consistently recorded and accumulated. If the rule changed, the $1 and $2 profits could not be compared.

Changes in consistency, if significant, need to be disclosed to the public. However, even insignificant inconsistencies can cause internal processing problems. For example, if there is a change in the method of recording orders, it could result in ordering excess inventory or not ordering enough.

Need for Consistency Controls

Consistency controls are needed to conform with generally accepted accounting principles and good business policy. Certified public accountants must confirm that data is consistent and state where it is not. Management needs consistency of data so that it can analyze current conditions and trends (see Exhibit 7.4).

Controls to Reduce Risks

Consistency is the basis of most computerized applications. One of the objectives of data processing is to achieve a consistency that is sometimes difficult to achieve in a manual system. The two risks that threaten consistency are the inability to translate needs into technical requirements and the inability to control technology.

Reducing the Inability to Translate Needs into Technical Requirements Risk. The major threat to consistency is the design of the system. If the user has not specified the types of consistency required, that consistency may not be built into the system. Systems designers should be made aware of the importance of consistency and include it in their systems plan.

Consistency controls should be primarily incorporated into the process and output functions of a system. As with other aspects of the application, the process function contains preventive controls, and the output function contains detective controls.

1. **Improving Process Control** Consistency means consistency of applying processing rules. These are the rules for determining in which accounting period data will be recorded and the rules for the recording and accumulation of data. Controls include:
   - *Transaction Dating* A date is placed in a transaction indicat-

Exhibit 7.4   Placing Consistency Controls Matrix

	Systems Function				
	Input	Process	Storage	Output	Use
EDP Risk[a]					
Inability to translate needs into technical requirements	2	3	2	3	1
Inability to control technology	2	3	2	2	3
Differences[b]					
Human functions replaced with machines	√	√			
Coded data not readable by people	√			√	√
Rapid processing		√		√	√
Errors preprogrammed		√		√	√
Automation of control	√	√	√	√	
Centralization of functions			√		√
New forms of evidence	√		√	√	√
New methods of authorization	√				√
New processing concepts	√	√	√	√	√

[a] 3 = high need for control, 2 = average need for control, 1 = low need for control.
[b] √ = difference affects control.

ing to which accounting period that transaction belongs. This enables the processing routines to easily determine to which accounting period the transaction belongs.
- *Generally Accepted Accounting Principles*   The requirements established by the accounting community must be followed.
2. **Improving Output Control**   There are two ways in which inconsistency can occur. One is the makeup of the data itself, and the other is the interpretation of that makeup as viewed by the user. Output controls can help ensure that the user understands the basis for which the data was prepared. Controls include:
   - *Report Descriptions*   A short description is placed in the front of a report, describing the basis by which the data was

collected. This tells the user of the report when the report was prepared, where the data came from, how complete it is, and so on.

- *Report Headings* Information is placed on each page, indicating the accounting period and other pertinent information to help the user use and understand the report.

Reducing the Inability to Control Technology Risk. Much of the consistency risk with technology is associated with data storage. If that data is not properly identified, the result can be inconsistency in data use. The inconsistency can be lessened by properly identifying data and making that identification known to the user.

1. **Improving Process Control** Diverse users have different interpretations of the consistency of data. This is particularly true when reliability is a factor in interpretation. In a previous example, we discussed why people being judged on the hours reported may report hours different from those actually worked in order to fall within the framework of their supervisor's expectations, instead of reporting reliably. Controls include *hardware monitors*, which are automatic data collection devices placed within the system. For example, job accounting systems, instead of pencil and paper, might monitor factory machines for production quantities and collect computer processing information. This control automates the monitoring process.

2. **Improving Use Control** Users must oversee the use of technology in their applications. Some of this can be done by monitoring, while other controls utilize redundancy. Controls include:

    - *Statistical Sampling* Take a sample of the output transactions to verify the consistency of processing.
    - *Audit* Have auditors evaluate the processing rules to determine that there are no consistency problems.

PLACING AUTHORIZATION CONTROLS

The environment can verify the security that determines that only authorized people gain access to data. However, the application must verify that those authorized people perform only authorized tasks. For example, a clerk in the payroll department may be authorized to change pay rates. However, that does not give that individual authority to change his or her own rate unless supervisors have approved it.

The systems analyst needs to recognize these two levels of authorization. One level is authorization to have access to change data, whereas the second level is the authorization from management to change a specific data element. One level can be controlled by the environment, but the other level must be controlled by the application.

Need for Authorization Controls

Authorization controls are both preventive and detective. They are preventive from the aspect that people who know controls exist are less likely to perform an unauthorized act they know will be detected. For example, it does no good to change your pay rate if it is detected before you get your next pay check. It is the detection aspect of authorization that helps prevent many unauthorized acts.

An organization has an obligation not to tempt its employees. Strong authorization detection controls eliminate the temptation to perform unauthorized acts (see Exhibit 7.5).

Controls to Reduce Risks

The risks that threaten authorization include the inability to translate needs into technical requirements, concentration of responsibilities, and incorrect entry of data. In addition, there are the normal threats of fraud and embezzlement. However, good controls that lessen the risks associated with computer technology also lessen the fraud and embezzlement risks. Although this book does not deal specifically with fraud and embezzlement, systems analysts should be aware of those threats when designing authorization controls.

Reducing the Inability to Translate Needs into Technical Requirements Risk. The control of authorization should be both preventive and detective. It is important in achieving this control objective that proper evidence be retained so that unauthorized transactions can be corrected. The problems associated with translating needs into technical requirements primarily involve omissions. In other words, the system has not specified the second level of authorization control, which is management's approval to execute a specific transaction. Controls for this risk should be placed in the process and output functions of the system.

Exhibit 7.5 Placing Authorization Controls Matrix

	Systems Function				
	Input	Process	Storage	Output	Use
EDP Risk[a]					
Inability to translate needs into technical requirements	2	3	2	3	1
Concentration of responsibilities	1	1	3	1	3
Incorrect entry of data	3	3	1	2	3
Differences[b]					
Human functions replaced with machines	√	√			
Coded data not readable by people	√			√	√
Rapid processing		√		√	√
Errors preprogrammed		√		√	√
Automation of control	√	√	√	√	
Centralization of functions			√		√
New forms of evidence	√		√	√	√
New methods of authorization	√				√
New processing concepts	√	√	√	√	√

[a] 3 = high need for control, 2 = average need for control, 1 = low need for control.
[b] √ = difference affects control.

1. **Improving Process Control** The process function can help prevent unauthorized changes by limiting the capabilities of people to make them. Controls include *granularity of processing*, which restricts the amount of change an individual can make to a specific data element. For example, the pay rate field change might be limited to a range of plus or minus 10%.

2. **Improving Output Control** The computer application can generate output messages questioning the authority to make a change. This obviously would not stop fraudulent acts, but would help prevent many erroneous unauthorized acts. Controls

include *warning messages*, which question the authorization to perform an act. This permits an individual to investigate and reverse the act if appropriate.

Reducing the Concentration of Responsibilities Risk. When one individual or a group of individuals has too much responsibility, there is the temptation to perform unauthorized acts. This temptation is encouraged by weak controls. The easiest method to overcome this temptation is to develop strong controls that lessen the temptation risk. These controls are best applied in the data storage and use functions.

1. **Improving Data Storage Control** Information contained in data storage provides the evidence needed to detect unauthorized acts. This evidence should be used as both a preventive and a detective measure to lessen the temptation when responsibilities are concentrated. Systems analysts should recognize that responsibilities will be concentrated, and they should design controls to lessen those risks. Controls include *employee account monitoring*, or reviewing accounts established in the name of an employee, such as employee savings accounts, payroll accounts, and charge accounts, for possible misuse.

2. **Improving Use Control** User personnel should monitor potential misuse of their own application. This can be done by maintaining controls over what has been authorized and by monitoring so that no other such events occur. Controls include:

   - *Questionable Transaction Verification* Provide a supervisor a list of questionable transactions, such as all credits given to customers, performed by subordinates.
   - *Independent Reconciliation* Have an independent party verify the correctness of processing. For example, a checking account should be reconciled by a party other than those drawing and signing checks.

Reducing the Incorrect Entry of Data Risk. One method of unauthorized processing is incorrect entry of data. If the data initiating the transaction is erroneous, obviously the transaction is not authorized. These transactions can be processed accurately and completely, but be unauthorized. Because of the pervasiveness of errors in data processing systems, preventive, detective, and corrective controls should be used.

1. **Improving Input Control** The input function should prevent the incorrect entry of data, incorrect being used in the sense that it is not an authorized transaction. One reason for incorrect data is the duplicate entry of that data. Controls include:

   - *Transaction Sequence Number* Sequentially number all transactions so that a duplicate entry of a transaction (i.e., two transactions with the same number) would be caught.
   - *Prenumbering Input* Use prenumbered forms so that all input transactions are uniquely identified, enabling the system to monitor for duplicates.

2. **Improving Process Control** The process function can use data in storage to verify the authenticity of input data. Controls include:

   - *Master Verification* The data entered to update master records is verified to determine whether it is from an authorized source. For example, who enters changes to the pay rate field on the payroll master, can be verified in this way.
   - *Limit Checks* These checks verify that a transaction does not exceed a predetermined authorized limit. For example, a customer's purchase can't exceed his or her credit limit.

3. **Improving Use Control** The user should be continually on guard for incorrect data. Once processing has been completed, it is sometimes difficult to make corrections. Controls include *document voiding*, that is, cancelling input documents so they will not be reentered and cancelling voided output forms, such as checks, so they cannot be erroneously used.

SUMMARY

The appliation has the primary control responsibility for completeness, accuracy, consistency, and authorization of data. These control responsibilities apply to data. However, that data is processed in a control environment. If that environment is not adequately controlled, then additional controls must be established in the application to compensate for control environment weaknesses.

In designing application controls, the systems designer should first assess the adequacy of the control environment. It is the combination of the environmental and application controls that determine the adequacy of control over the data.

CHAPTER 8

Using Controls to Improve Performance

Controls can be used to direct an operation to a successful conclusion in addition to preventing, detecting, and correcting problems. Controls help make organizations profitable. For example, critical path planning helps large projects to be completed on time. This positive aspect of control is often overlooked.

Operational controls should also help provide assurance that the system meets the needs of the user. We would think that users would inform data processing personnel when a computer system meets or fails to meet their needs. But this does not always happen, and the reasons are numerous. Among them are the fact that users do not know what they get, do not appreciate the interrelationship of their and others' systems, and in many cases just don't care what the system does. Many users have the attitude that the system "belongs" to data processing and not to them.

Operational controls are normally system-oriented controls. Their purpose is to ensure that the system meets the user's needs in a cost-effective manner. These controls help assure management that the goals and objectives are being achieved. If not, the controls alert management to potential problems so corrective action can be taken.

Operational controls should be built into

systems as the systems are designed. This chapter examines the operational risks, identifies the phase in the system development life cycle (SDLC) where those risks should be addressed, and then describes some examples of control that are effective in reducing those risks.

Computerized business applications should be designed so they are cost-effective. This is an important aspect of computer systems design. Controls should be used to help in the development and operation of cost-effective systems. There are three considerations in cost-effectiveness: economy, effectiveness, and efficiency. All three are important in designing cost-effective computer systems.

SYSTEM DEVELOPMENT LIFE CYCLE (SDLC)

The SDLC is a systematic process for designing, implementing, and operating computerized business applications. The concept was developed to optimize the use of data processing resources. There is no commonly accepted SDLC. Companies have adopted variations of it for their own benefit and have modified it to meet the methods that they want to use in their operations.

The SDLC can be used in a strong or weak management environment. In a strong management environment, each phase of the SDLC is a management checkpoint. At the completion of each phase of the SDLC, management decides whether the system should move to the next phase. Experience has shown that heavy management involvement results in the development of effective systems.

It has become apparent to many managers that once a computer project is approved, it is almost impossible to abort. Once management approves the resources for the project, work progresses using an approach that makes it difficult to accurately pinpoint the status until the project is complete. If at completion the project fails to meet specifications, the entire investment might be lost. Management thus reasons that the only practical way to abort a poor project is to closely monitor the project during its development. If resources are only authorized through the completion of one SDLC phase, then management can easily stop the project when those resources are exhausted. Weaker management leaves the SDLC concept to the systems designers.

Management involvement in the SDLC enables management to ensure that adequate operational controls are installed in systems. The number of phases in the SDLC range from 4 to approximately 15.

For the purposes of explaining control, six phases are used. The phases are (see Figure 8.1):

• *Feasibility* Determines whether the needs can be satisfied by a computer system and considers the economics for developing and operating the system.

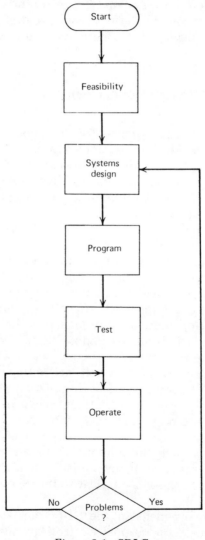

Figure 8.1 **SDLC.**

- *Systems Design* Includes cost/benefit analysis and translates the needs into specifications that can be programmed for a computer.
- *Program* Translates the design specifications into machine instructions.
- *Test* Verifies that the implemented system achieves the design specifications.
- *Operate* Executes the program using production data to satisfy users' needs.
- *Feedback (Problem Detection)* Continually monitors the system for problems to determine whether changes need to be made (this is normally called the maintenance or enhancements phase, but from a control viewpoint it is the isolation and correction of system and/or business problems).

Within each phase of the SDLC is the opportunity to reduce operational risks. The controls are needed to reduce the risks that prevent the system's tasks from being performed efficiently, effectively, and economically, and prevent the system from meeting the needs of the user. Each risk should be addressed in specific phases of the SDLC.

EDP RISKS/SDLC MATRIX

Operational performance of a computerized business application is achieved as a result of many tradeoffs. The types of controls selected partially depend on the tradeoff decisions. The systems analyst must weight these tradeoffs in attempting to optimize performance.

The more common tradeoffs the analyst faces in attempting to achieve optimal performance include:

- *Efficiency versus Economy* The efficient way to design a system may be quick and easy but not economical. The analyst frequently must choose between efficiency and economy in systems design.
- *Size and Scope of Project versus Staffing* If one person could design the entire system, he or she would know the intricacies of every program and every part of the system. This would enable that individual to build each part of the system knowing every other part. When a second person is assigned to the project team, that knowledge must be divided between the two people. Although there will be communication, neither one will be as

familiar with all the tasks being performed as when they are performed by one person. Thus a communication gap and a potential source for problems exist. When a third person is added, the problem is magnified, and so on.

- *Quality of System versus Cost to Build*   If the most skilled senior people are assigned to a project and given all the time they desire to complete the project, the result should be a superbly constructed system. Unfortunately, the cost may make the system prohibitive. Lowering the cost of building the system is normally a tradeoff with quality.

- *Meeting Schedules and Budgets versus Testing*   If a system undergoes sufficient testing, all the major bugs should be detected. Unfortunately, testing is a time-consuming, costly aspect of systems development. When the needed testing is reduced to save money or time, the lack of testing increases the risk of problems.

- *Proven versus New Technology*   If the systems analyst uses known technology, there should be few technological problems. However, by doing this the analyst may deny the user the advantages of newer but yet unproven technology.

- *Documentation versus Personal Knowledge*   A strong control is extensive documentation. This documentation is developed during every phase of the SDLC. However, documentation is costly to develop and maintain, and much of the information that could be documented is already present in the experience of the project team. The project team may not need documentation to adequately maintain, test, and extend the system. The analyst faces the dilemma of how much to rely on the experience of the project team and how much formal documentation is needed to protect the integrity of the system.

- *Automated Tasks versus Human Tasks*   Tasks can be performed either by people or machines. The systems analyst must determine which tasks can be done best by people and which by machines. Errors in placements result in poor systems performance.

Whichever side of the tradeoff the analyst selects, there are risks. However, when the analyst is familiar with the tradeoff and the risks involved, controls can be established to minimize those risks. For example, if inexperienced people are chosen to lower the drain on skilled resources, then a control of increased supervision is warranted.

The risks that are unique to or increased in a computerized business environment that threaten operational performance include

Exhibit 8.1 EDP Risks/SDLC Matrix

		SDLC				
EDP Risk[a]	Feasibility	Systems Design	Program	Test	Operate	Feedback
Improper use of technology	1	3	2	1	1	3
Inability to react quickly	1	3	1	1	3	2
Inability to translate needs into technical requirements	3	3	2	1	1	2
Inability to control technology	1	3	3	3	3	2

[a]3 = high need for control, 2 = average need for control, 1 = low need for control.

161

the improper use of technology, the inability to react quickly, the inability to translate needs into technical requirements, and the inability to control technology. These risks and their placement in the proper phase for solution during the SDLC are illustrated in Exhibit 8.1.

Reducing Operational Risks

The analyst should attempt to build the best possible system at the minimum cost. Each time the analyst compromises on quality, or is exorbitant on cost, the systems analyst is not fulfilling his or her responsibility.

This chapter provides the analyst the same approach for designing operational controls as that discussed in the environmental and application control chapters. The EDP risks/SDLC matrix (see Exhibit 8.1) shows the interrelationship between the risks and the various phases of the SDLC. A 3 indicates a high need for control design during that phase, a 2 indicates an average need for control, and a 1 a low need for control. Controls should be designed during the phases indicated with a 3.

Some of the recommended controls are over the design process as opposed to being built into the application. In those instances, controlling the process helps reduce the risk. For example, having users certify that they believe the controls are adequate forces the users to review the adequacy of the controls in their applications.

As these risks are related to each of the SDLC phases, the differences that cause the risks are identified. The differences part of the matrix shows those areas of a computerized business application that are different from a noncomputerized application. After the analyst determines where there is high need for control, the analyst should design and place controls to reduce those risks. Knowing the differences can be helpful in selecting the proper control. The analyst can do this by examining the differences and then designing controls that will minimize those differences.

Operational Control Objectives

The control objectives to be achieved for operational performance are efficiency, effectiveness, economy, and meeting the needs of the users. These control objectives themselves are frequently tradeoff situations and therefore are discussed individually. For example, the efficient way to transmit information may be over communication lines. However, it may not be the most economical way. Therefore, the analyst would be concerned with the efficiency verus economy tradeoff.

A matrix is provided for each of the operational control objectives. Each matrix shows the risks, the phases of the SDLC, and the differences between a computerized and noncomputerized environment.

PLACING EFFICIENCY CONTROLS

Efficiency is the ease by which tasks can be performed. However, efficiency does not mean that the tasks are performed effectively or economically. Efficiency implies a reduction in either the effort or number of steps required to accomplish a task.

An efficient programmer normally has the least number of compiles and the least number of tests. An efficient systems analyst may ask for only a minimum amount of user personnel time. An efficient operation of a system on the computer will have a minimum number of file changes.

As systems analysts evaluate efficiency, they must weight efficiency against economy and effectiveness. For example, a programmer may be efficient in the number of computer compilations per program, but the procedures used for that efficiency may affect the effectiveness and economy of the programming function. It may be necessary to do large amounts of desk debugging, flowcharting, and documentation to cut the number of program compiles to a minimum. These extra steps may require more programmer time than is saved by reducing the number of compilations. The extra programmer time may actually extend the programming schedule, which reduces the effectiveness of the project team.

Management must be continually aware that people perform tasks according to the manner by which they are judged. For example, if a programmer is judged on the number of compilations used in developing a program, that programmer will minimize the number of compilations. Economy, effectiveness, and efficiency are tradeoffs in the performance of the data processing function. When designing, implementing, and evaluating the results of operational controls, these tradeoffs must be considered. The control examples in this chapter will provide some guidance for improving operational performance.

Need for Efficiency Controls

Efficiency is normally learned from experience. When people perform tasks incorrectly they should learn the right way to accomplish them or at least a way that should not be repeated. For example, programmers learned years ago that trying to write programs using the least number of instructions was not an efficient way to program. Today's programmer looks at program efficiency from the writing, operating, and maintaining perspectives instead of being concerned only about minimizing program codes.

Controls to Reduce Risks

Losses due to ineffective operational controls are normally the loss of data processing resources, which can be a loss of people time, computer time, or performance in the user area. All result in the loss of resources to the organization, which may be a more serious loss than some weaknesses in the application area.

Efficiency controls direct the expenditure of data processing resources. The controls primarily utilize experience gained from previous efforts. Many of these lessons may have been costly, and controls should ensure that the same mistakes are not made over and over again.

The following controls should help reduce the probability of loss due to the risks threatening efficiency. These controls are listed as examples of the types of controls that can be used in achieving the efficiency control objective. They are not meant to be a comprehensive list but, rather, a guide to systems analysts as to the type of controls that are effective (see Exhibit 8.2).

Reducing the Improper Use of Technology Risk. Failure to understand the technology normally results in inefficient use of that technology. Prior to the installation of technology, the organization should gain a full understanding of the advantages and disadvantages of that technology and formulate a plan for its efficient use.

The two phases in the SDLC to install controls over technology are systems design and feedback. Controls in the systems design phase help prevent inefficient use of technology; controls in the feedback phase detect the inefficient use of technology.

Exhibit 8.2 Placing of Efficiency Controls Matrix

		SDLC				
	Feasibility	Systems Design	Program	Test	Operate	Feedback
EDP Risk[a]						
Improper use of technology	1	3	2	1	1	3
Inability to control technology	1	3	3	3	3	2
Differences[b]						
Human functions replaced with machines	✓	✓				✓
Coded data not readable by people		✓				✓
Rapid processing		✓	✓	✓	✓	✓
Errors preprogrammed		✓	✓	✓	✓	✓
Automation of control		✓	✓	✓	✓	✓
Centralization of functions	✓	✓				
New forms of evidence	✓	✓				✓
New methods of authorization	✓	✓				✓
New processing concepts	✓	✓	✓	✓	✓	✓

[a] 3 = high need for control, 2 = average need for control, 1 = low need for control.
[b] ✓ = difference affects control.

1. **Improving Systems Design Phase Control** The proper preparation for the use of technology is the best control to ensure its efficient use. Controls include:

   - *Technology Selection Group* Appoint a group of senior systems analysts to oversee the selection and implementation of computer hardware and software. This group should be knowledgeable in the needs of the organization and can select technology accordingly.

   - *Hardware and Software Standards* Establish standards to be followed by systems analysts in the use of hardware and software. This eliminates repeating costly mistakes.

2. **Improving Feedback Phase Control** Monitoring how technology is used provides information on how efficiently or inefficiently the technology is being utilized. Controls include:

   - *Job Accounting Systems* Software monitors provided by vendors measure the use of hardware (e.g., IBM's systems management facility) record hardware, file, and other system resource usage. Job accounting systems can also charge users for the resources they consumed.

   - *Technology Update Manuals* Hardware and software reports on the performance of technology, provided by independent evaluation groups (e.g., the technology evaluation manual provided by AUERBACH), draw on the experiences of other users in assessing the capabilities of technology.

Reducing the Inability to Control Technology Risk. Many of the problems associated with the inefficient use of technology are due to the lack of controls. To control the use of technology, an organization needs information to monitor its use. Controls incorporated in the major phases of the SDLC provide management with this information.

The inability to control technology applies to all phases of the SDLC. Controls need to be installed in each of the SDLC phases to prevent technical problems from progressing to the next phase.

1. **Improving Systems Design Phase Control** Controls in the systems design phase should ensure that an efficient systems design is prepared. Controls include:

   - *Quality Assurance Function* An independent group of experts evaluates the design prior to the programming phase.

This group determines that standards are followed and specifications are implemented.

- *Security Officer Function* The security officer is responsible for establishing and enforcing security policy. Among the tasks performed is the development of security profiles indicating who can have access to which data processing resources.

2. **Improving Program Phase Control** Controls in the program phase should ensure that the program is put together efficiently. Controls include *structured programming*, an orderly method of building programs so that all pieces fit together. This method improves documentation and normally reduces maintenance effort.

3. **Improving Test Phase Control** Programmers normally want to minimize the number of tests required because testing is not the most challenging part of their job. Controls should ensure that the maximum utilization of each test is achieved. Controls include:

- *Full Testing* Tests should not be stopped in the middle, but run to completion so that the maximum number of conditions can be examined during each test run.
- *Automatic Tracing* The trace option of programming languages should be incorporated if available so that the programmer has the maximum amount of information back from each test. Tracing shows what paths in a program were followed, which helps pinpoint the source of problems should they occur.

4. **Improving Operate Phase Control** Controls should ensure that the operational efficiency of a program does not degrade over a period of time. Controls include *transaction timing*, which is monitoring the amount of time required to process a transaction. This time to process a transaction should be plotted over a period of time as an indicator of when programs start to become inefficient. An increasingly longer span for processing a transaction is indicative of processing problems.

PLACING EFFECTIVENESS CONTROLS

Effectiveness is performing tasks in such a manner that the stated objectives are achieved. Data processing people usually refer to needs in the context of specified as opposed to actual needs, because they

attempt to implement what is specified. Frequently there is a difference. Meeting the actual needs is discussed in the "Meets-User Needs"
section of this chapter. Effectiveness is the ease in which specified
needs are achieved.

Many times the policies and procedures of an organization reduce
its effectiveness. For example, a common experience is being in a
department store and finding that one sales clerk with no customers
cannot take your order, making you wait in line until an overworked
sales clerk can take your order. From a sales viewpoint, this does not
appear to the customer to be an effective way to run a store.

Effectiveness must be measured in terms of how well specific tasks
are performed. When viewed from this perspective, effectiveness
does not mean the most efficient way to perform a task. For example, top management of an organization may worry that customers
will receive too many credits from the sales department because the
sales department wants satisfied customers more than it wants
profits. To offset this concern, the controller may require three
approval signatures before a credit can be issued. From the controller's perspective, this is effective because it minimizes the credits
issued. However, all recognize that it is not an efficient way to issue
credits because so many people are involved with the associated time
delays.

Technology poses a threat to systems effectiveness. At the same
time, new technology is offering solutions to the ineffective processing methods of the past. For example, overnight batch processing
was not an effective way to run banking systems. The use of on-line
data base systems has enabled tellers to substantially speed up the
banking process. No longer must they pull signature cards and
account balance cards; rather, they can get the necessary information quickly over communication lines. Customers can enter "secret"
passwords, which eliminates the need to pull signature cards.

The airline reservation systems were becoming too cumbersome
for the number of air travelers. Newer technology enabling on-line
inquiry and reservation confirmation revolutionized the airline
industry. However, these technological advances also have problems.

Need for Effectiveness Controls

Over time, people learn how to use and control technology effectively. They learn that the most efficient and most economical way
of using technology is not always the best way. Effectiveness implies

the best way of accomplishing a task from a user perspective. Unfortunately, the cost of inefficiency of operations may make alternative methods preferable.

Building the proper controls helps assure management that computer technology will be used effectively. The threats to the best use of technology are the improper use of technology and the inability to control technology. It is also through controls that management can be assured of the effective use of the data processing resources.

Controls to Reduce Risks

Effective implies establishing and using standards and procedures learned over a period of time. If these standards and procedures are formalized, continually improved, and enforced, the data processing resources tend to be used effectively (see Exhibit 8.3).

Reducing the Improper Use of Technology Risk. One of the dangers is that technology will be used for technology's sake. Data processing personnel often look for places to use new technology, as opposed to determining the most effective way to meet a user's needs. Controls to ensure that this doesn't happen are best placed in the systems design and feedback phases of the SDLC.

1. **Improving Systems Design Phase Control** Management should guard against a mismatch between satisfying needs and using new technology. Many organizations have concluded that data base technology was introduced into their organization before the need for that technology existed. Controls to reduce this probability include:
    *   *Systems Design Alternatives* Data processing personnel should be forced to provide evaluations of the various alternatives available for solving a problem. The alternatives should always include modifying the existing system. Even if the economics are slanted, the alternatives are still covered for management probing.
    *   *Business Systems Solution* This requires solving the business problem prior to determining how to implement the solution, which avoids developing a solution that may not solve the primary business problem.
2. **Improving Feedback Phase Control** Providing management with sufficient feedback information quickly pinpoints the ineffective

Exhibit 8.3 Placing Effectiveness Controls Matrix

EDP Risk[a]	Feasibility	Systems Design	Program	Test	Operate	Feedback
Improper use of technology	1	3	2	1	1	3
Inability to control technology	1	3	3	3	3	2
Differences[b]						
Human functions replaced with machines	✓	✓				✓
Coded data not readable by people		✓				✓
Rapid processing		✓	✓	✓	✓	✓
Errors preprogrammed		✓	✓	✓	✓	✓
Automation of control		✓	✓	✓	✓	✓
Centralization of functions	✓	✓				✓
New forms of evidence	✓	✓				✓
New methods of authorization	✓	✓				✓
New processing concepts	✓	✓	✓	✓	✓	✓

[a] 3 = high need for control, 2 = average need for control, 1= low need for control.
[b] √ = difference affects control.

use of technology. Although it may be too late to economically correct the system, the lessons learned can be transposed to new systems so the same error will not be repeated. Controls include *postinstallation audit*, which is an evaluation shortly after a new system or major change goes operational that measures the accomplishment versus systems design criteria. This determines whether the needs have been met and the system functions as specified.

Reducing the Inability to Control Technology Risk. Controls can help ensure that technology will be used properly. In an environment where controls over the effective use of technology do not exist, management cannot be sure how well its technical experts are performing. Controls in this area are a means of measuring the performance of an organization's data processing personnel.

The feasibility phase is highly creative and one in which it is difficult to measure effectiveness. It is also a phase where only minimal resources are used, and the results should stand on their own merits. However, the systems design, program, test, and operate phases need effectiveness controls.

1. **Improving Systems Design Phase Control** The systems design tasks are partly creative and partly structured. However, a systems designer's creativity should remain within the structured process. Controls include:
   - *Structured Design* This effective and orderly technique for designing systems normally begins by specifying user output needs and then working backward to source data in an effort to fulfill those needs.
   - *Quality Assurance Review* Independent experts review the effectiveness of the systems design to determine that the developmental standards and procedures have been followed.
2. **Improving Program Phase Control** The programming process should be a production-type operation if programs have been adequately specified. Controls on the effectiveness of programmers include *program writing standards*, or criteria against which to measure programming performance. These standards include such things as expected numbers of compiles and hours of effort per programming statement.
3. **Improving Test Phase Control** Testing is one of the more difficult aspects of computer systems effort. It is one of the least automated and frequently depends on how well the program was

designed. Controls include *problems logging*. After the programmer has indicated that the program is correct, records should be
maintained of the number and types of problems uncovered. The
records help identify people who do not adequately test their
programs and identify common programming problems so corrective action can be taken.

4. **Improving Operate Phase Control** Effectiveness in computer
   operations measures the effectiveness of both the systems design
   and the computer operations personnel. Controls over operations
   include:

   - *Restart and Recovery Logs* A recording and evaluation of
     the number of times and reasons for restart and recovery
     operations identify common problems as well as individual
     operator problems.
   - *User Complaints* The number of times and the reasons the
     user is unsatisfied with the results of computer operations,
     which includes timeliness of delivery of reports, should be
     recorded and evaluated.

PLACING ECONOMY CONTROLS

The private sector must show a profit to continue operations. The
public sector must operate within budgets approved by the legisla-
ture. Budgets place restrictions on the amount of funds that can be
used to operate the data processing resources.

How economically a data processing group can function may
determine its success. However, effectiveness is normally the primary
criterion, and economy is second. It is of little value to do a job
economically that is not effective in meeting the stated needs of
the user.

Economy can be measured by many yardsticks. Among the ones
commonly used are:

- *Current Cost versus Prior Cost* If the new system costs less
  money than the old system, it is judged economical.
- *Cost Avoidance* Increased costs can be avoided because of system capabilities.
- *Stabilized Cost* If a system can be installed, and the volume of
  transactions can be increased without significantly affecting costs,
  the system can be considered economical.

- *System Flexibility* The system can be easily adjusted or modified. For example, new prices or sales tax rates can be easily
  installed and volumes or frequency of runs can be changed with
  minimal inconvenience.
- *Actual versus Budget* If a project is allocated fixed amount of
  dollars to implement or operate and does it for fewer dollars, it is
  termed an economical system.
- *Prior Labor versus Current Labor Cost* If a new system can
  eliminate people who were previously required to perform a
  function, it may be considered an economical system.

This list includes only some of the many ways by which economy
is measured. What is economical in one person's mind may not be
economical in another's. Therefore, a systems analyst must have a
good understanding of what is meant by an economical system in
his or her organization and then attempt to build such a system.

It may prove beneficial for a data processing department to establish the criteria against which economy can be measured. Data
processing, like many professional fields, is an area where it is
difficult to measure economical performance. Establishing performance criteria can help overcome this problem. For example, if
one line of coding per hour for a programmer is a programming
standard, then if a project can exceed that standard, for example,
code one line every 50 minutes, then the installation can be considered economical.

Need for Economy Controls

Without controls, management cannot evaluate the economy of performance of the data processing function. Controls not only provide
the yardstick for measurement, but also help enforce those yardsticks. Good controls can help make the operations of the data
processing department more economical.

Economy, effectiveness, and efficiency are all related to standards.
Standards help establish the procedures, provide direction for people
in the performance of their tasks, and can be used to measure
performance.

Controls to Reduce Risks

There are two risks that threaten economical operations: the improper use of technology and the inability to control technology.

These same risks apply to all operational controls. However, the risks can be reduced through controls (see Exhibit 8.4).

Reducing the Improper Use of Technology Risk.   Large amounts of resources can be wasted quickly through the improper use of technology. It is not uncommon to run systems again and again without proper diagnoses of problems. Often there is a tendency to do things hastily or place the burden for problem diagnosis on others (e.g., the vendor), without undertaking the proper planning and diagnostic steps that would ensure economical use of the equipment. Controls in the systems design and feedback phases can help ensure the economical use of technology.

1. **Improving Systems Design Controls** The system design process should solve the business problem first and select technology second. This approach tends to minimize installing new technology prior to its need. Controls include:
    * *Business System SDLC Phase*   Establishing a separate phase in the SDLC to concentrate on solving the business problem reduces the probability of introducing new technology and then looking for a problem to solve using that technology.
    * *Technology Standards* Developing standards that encourage good practices and discourage bad practices aid in the proper use of technology. The standards should be based on the experiences of the organization in using technology, and then continually modified to reflect newly uncovered good practices, and bad practices.
2. **Improving Feedback Phase Controls** Feedback controls should continually monitor the performance of technology. Without continuous monitoring conditions can change that degrade performance, and those conditions may not be detected. Controls include:
    * *Software Metrics* Metrics use the relationship of two variables to predict the performance of technology. For example, the relationships in programs between the number of program statements to the number of complex and compound program statements help predict the ease or difficulty of maintaining that program.
    * *Hardware Metrics* The relationship, for example, between operational hours per month and down time predicts the reliability of hardware.

Exhibit 8.4 Placing Economical Controls Matrix

			SDLC			
	Feasibility	Systems Design	Program	Test	Operate	Feedback
EDP Risk[a]						
Improper use of technology	1	3	2	1	1	3
Inability to control technology	1	3	3	3	3	2
Differences[b]						
Human functions replaced with machines	✓	✓				✓
Coded data not readable by people		✓				✓
Rapid processing		✓	✓	✓	✓	✓
Errors preprogrammed		✓	✓	✓	✓	✓
Automation of control		✓	✓	✓	✓	✓
Centralization of functions	✓	✓				✓
New forms of evidence	✓	✓				✓
New methods of authorization	✓	✓				✓
New processing concepts	✓	✓	✓	✓	✓	✓

[a] 3 = high need for control, 2 = average need for control, 1 = low need for control.
[b] ✓ = difference affects control.

- *Mapping* This process identifies unused program code as well as the frequency of use of individual program instructions, which indicates the areas of programs that could be deleted or, if improved, may increase the efficiency of the program.

Reducing the Inability to Control Technology Risk. The use of automated technology can substantially reduce the cost per unit of work. However, if the technology is not adequately controlled, the result may be higher costs. The control of technology requires people who understand both control and the technology to implement the procedures that provide assurance that the technology is utilized in the most economical manner.

1. **Improving Systems Design Phase Control** Planning is normally the key to economical operations. When people know what they are doing, they usually do it economically. Controls include:
   - *Project Evaluation Review Technique (PERT)* PERT pinpoints problems quickly before resources are wasted unnecessarily. This shows the steps, and order of the steps, that must be executed to implement a project.
   - *Management by Objective (MBO)* MBO establishes economy objectives for the project team to meet. This control defines for each individual what he or she is to do and provides a yardstick by which management can judge the individual's performance.
2. **Improving Program Phase Control** Implementing the systems design specifications most economically is a task that also requires planning. Frequently, the existing applications can do the job, but some extensive changes may be made without proper analysis of the problem. Controls include:
   - *Utilizing Vendor System Features* Using the features provided by vendors in their software and hardware may eliminate special coding (e.g., DBMS's frequently include automatic edits, thus eliminating the need for audit programs). Too frequently organizations develop a routine that is available at minimal or no cost from a vendor because it is not their practice to use vendor routines.
   - *Data Base* Maintaining data independently of the programs enables large segments of what normally requires special coding to be accomplished using features provided by the data base technology. Using this concept, data can be controlled

independently of the programmer, which can both improve control and automate large segments of systems design.

3. **Improving Test Phase Control** Testing should obtain the maximum assurance that there are no bugs in the system, so when the system becomes operational problems will be minimal. Controls to help ensure this include:

   - *Acceptance Testing* Involving the people, who will actually use the system after it becomes operational, in the testing. These are the people who know how the system should work and thus are in a better position than data processing personnel to identify problems.
   - *Testing Criteria* Determining the acceptable level of performance prior to placing a system into production. Unless people know the criteria that must be achieved from testing, they cannot conduct tests in a businesslike manner.

4. **Improving Operate Phase Control** Computer operations personnel should develop procedures to permit the economical operation of all systems. These controls include:

   - *Monitoring Operations* In on-line operations scheduling may not be practical; therefore, operations must be monitored so that adjustments can be made to facilitate the smooth flow of work.
   - *Scheduling* An orderly scheduling of jobs eliminates the need for rush and special handling in running jobs.
   - *Operation Documentation* Formally documented procedures to operate each system help eliminate operator mistakes. This documentation provides a step-by-step method for running each job and each operating function, such as recovery.

PLACING MEETS USER NEEDS CONTROLS

Nothing is more discouraging and frustrating to data processing personnel than to develop an economical, effective, and efficient computer system that is rejected by the user. This failure to meet the needs of the user has cost many data processing people their jobs and has caused others to quit an organization in complete frustration. The prospects of working one or more years on a project and having it discarded is devastating.

The inability to meet user needs has many causes. Included among the causes are:

- *Communication Problems* The user and systems analyst are not able to communicate with each other.
- *User Inability to State Needs* Many users cannot articulate what they want accomplished in detail sufficient for a systems analyst to design a system to meet the real needs.
- *Needs Unknown* The user doesn't know what is needed at the start of the systems development process.
- *Overengineering* The system developed is too complex to be used by user personnel.
- *Overbudget and Late* Excessive cost and late installation result in the lack of users' confidence in the ability of the system to meet their needs.
- *Sabotage* User personnel are upset by the prospects of a new system and intentionally and unintentionally take whatever steps are necessary to destroy the system.
- *Misuse of Technology* Technology is used that cannot meet the needs of the user (e.g., response time is too long or too little output is provided).
- *Inadequate Data Processing Skills* The data processing personnel assigned to the project do not have skills sufficient to build the needed system.
- *Technological Problems* The technology does not function properly, causing the inability either to get the system operational or to keep the system operational.

As with other operational control objectives, the meets user needs objective requires planning and coordination with user personnel. Many of the efforts undertaken by the data processing profession to ensure user satisfaction involve user personnel. Data processing personel have continually lobbied for more user involvement in systems development. When users are involved, the satisfaction rate normally increases.

Need for Meets User Needs Controls

Without sufficient controls, new systems and extensions to existing systems may not meet user needs. When this happens, systems are either aborted or changed. Both are costly in terms of dollars and waste of human abilities. Most of the failure to meet user needs can be overcome with proper controls (see Exhibit 8.5).

Exhibit 8.5   Placing Meets User Needs Controls Matrix

		SDLC				
	Feasibility	Systems Design	Program	Test	Operate	Feedback
EDP Risk[a]						
Improper use of technology	1	3	2	1	1	3
Inability to react quickly	1	3	1	1	3	2
Inability to translate needs into technical requirements	3	3	2	1	1	2
Inability to control technology	1	3	3	3	3	2
Differences[b]						
Human functions replaced with machines	✓	✓				✓
Coded data not readable by people		✓				✓
Rapid processing		✓	✓	✓	✓	✓
Error preprogrammed		✓	✓	✓	✓	✓
Automation of control		✓	✓	✓	✓	✓
Centralization of functions	✓	✓				✓
New forms of evidence	✓	✓		✓		✓
New methods of authorization	✓	✓				✓
New processing concepts	✓	✓	✓	✓	✓	✓

[a] 3 = high need for control, 2 = average need for control, 1 = low need for control.
[b] ✓ = difference affects control.

179

Controls to Reduce Risks

Organizations face four risks that threaten meeting user needs. These risks are the improper use of technology, the inability to react quickly, the inability to translate needs into technical requirements, and the inability to control technology. Incorporating controls into the SDLC reduces these risks.

Reducing the Improper Use of Technology Risk. The misuse of technology can cause systems not to meet user needs. The causes are both under- and overengineering. If the system does not have the sufficient hardware and software, it probably cannot meet the needs, and, if too much technology is used, the system may overwhelm user personnel. The most effective phases to install technology controls are systems design and feedback.

1. **Improving Systems Design Phase Control** Controls need to be established to assure management that the proper technology is being used to meet user requirements. Controls include:
   - *Quality Assurance Review* The technology plan is reviewed by independent experts to assess whether technology is being properly utilized.
   - *User Groups* Organizations meet with one another to discuss the technology they used to solve similar user problems. Most major vendors have user groups that offer organizations the opportunity to meet and discuss common problems with technology.
2. **Improving Feedback Phase Control** Feedback measures the use of technology against standards. Controls include:
   - *Technology Performance Standards* Standards are used to measure the performance of technology against organizational requirements. For example, an on-line response time standard might be a two-second response.
   - *System Change Evaluation* Evaluating the type of change requests, made by the user, to determine whether they are attributable to the improper use of technology.

Reducing the Ability to React Quickly Risk. Users have practical needs to solve. If the computer application cannot provide them with the information when needed, users will develop alternate methods of getting that information. When this happens, it means the computerized application does not meet their needs. Controls to reduce this risk should be installed in the systems design and operate phases.

1. **Improving Systems Design Phase Control** An organization's success may be based on the ability to react to customer needs. The ability to react may be based on information received from computer systems. Controls to evaluate this risk include:
   - *Customer Complaints Analysis* The customer's dissatisfaction with service may be attributable to data processing. Customer and user complaints should be recorded, categorized, and analyzed.
   - *Program Change Evaluation* Review requests for program changes due to not getting information on a timely basis. The program change requests should be recorded, categorized, and analyzed.

2. **Improving Operate Phase Control** Computer operations are a service to users. It is computer operations' responsibility to provide results when requested. Controls here include:
   - *Report Delivery Analysis Logs* Logs should be maintained indicating the success computer operations is having in meeting or not meeting schedules for the delivery of reports. This log can be used to instigate corrective action when required.
   - *Trend Analysis* Measure turnaround performance on a trend basis to show whether computer operations is improving, staying the same, or becoming worse.

Reducing the Ability to Translate Needs into Technical Requirements Risk. The greatest threat to meeting user needs is not understanding them. Management can install controls that help ensure that user needs are understood. These controls are best established in the feasibility and systems design phases.

1. **Improving Feasibility Phase Control** Feasibility encompasses much of the overall planning for systems development. It is here that new ideas are formulated, priorities are established, and the overall framework is developed for satisfying user needs. Controls here include:
   - *Steering Committee* Committees composed of the major users of data processing are formed to establish priorities of work.

- *User Involvement* User personnel participates in the feasibility study to ensure that the results meet their needs.
- *User Billings* When users are charged with the cost of the systems design, the design performance is more likely to be evaluated on the effectiveness of the systems design team.

2. **Improving Systems Design Phase Control** At the completion of the systems design phase, the user needs should be completely specified. Therefore, at the conclusion of this phase, the user needs are either met or not. From this point on, management need only be assured that the design specifications are implemented as stated. Controls that help ensure that user needs are properly specified include:

- *User Signoff* Users are given the detailed specifications to determine if the specifications are what they want; if so, they must sign a statement so stating.
- *User Test Data* For test purposes, during the design phase users provide systems designers with examples of transactions and desired processing results. This shows the designers specifically what the user is expecting.

Reducing the Inability to Control Technology Risk. Problems with technology can sabotage good systems design specifications. Technological problems can prevent the users from getting the desired results. Management should install controls to ensure that technology cannot go astray. Controls need to be installed in the four main phases of the SDLC.

1. **Improving Systems Design Phase Control** Adequate controls should be placed on technology in the design phase to ensure that user needs will not be undermined. Controls include:

- *Backup Procedures* These methods of operating the system should hardware or software problems develop include the processes and tasks required to prepare to recover.
- *Data Backup* Duplicate copies of system data are maintained in the event files are lost or destroyed.

2. **Improving Program Phase Control** The inability to translate user needs into program codes can result in a continual series of problems that result in the failure to meet user needs. Controls to lessen this threat include *programming standards*, that is, requiring programmers to use proven methods of coding programs so that if problems occur, the probability will be that the cause is not faulty programming.

3. **Improving Test Phase Control** Testing is the means of ensuring that technology is under control. Controls include:

   - *Hardware Startup Checks* A series of startup diagnostics can determine that the hardware is functioning properly.
   - *Base Case Testing* Preparing an exhaustive set of test data that will test all aspects of the system can uncover problems.
   - *Disaster Testing* A disaster is simulated so that the disaster recovery procedures can be tested, determining that backup facilities work in the event of a disaster.

4. **Improving Operate Phase Control** The computer operation department has a responsibility to verify that the technology performs properly. Controls include:

   - *System Utilization Report* Information on the performance and use of computer hardware enables operations management to ascertain that the hardware is meeting their operational needs.
   - *Preventive Maintenance* Hardware maintained on a regular basis as opposed to waiting until a system failure occurs.
   - *Vendor Failure Logs* Maintain logs on vendor performance for maintenance and the causes of troubles requiring special vendor maintenance. This becomes the basis for requesting improved maintenance if necessary.

SUMMARY

Controls can be effectively utilized to increase the operational performance of an organization's data processing function. Controls help improve effectiveness, efficiency, and the economy of computer operations. Perhaps the most important value of controls is ensuring that user needs are satisfied. The implementation of operational controls will provide top management with the needed assurance that its data processing resources are being properly utilized. For this reason, management should become involved in establishing controls over the operational performance of the data processing department.

CHAPTER 9

Assessing the Effectiveness of Controls

To be effective, controls must be adjusted to meet changing conditions. If controls are not continually adjusted, they normally lose their effectiveness. Controls should be reviewed by the same continual maintenance process that is used for any other aspect of systems development.

When controls are not regularly adjusted, they can reduce the operational flow of data through a computerized business system. Controls in a computer system are similar to those of a system of traffic lights. When the traffic lights are properly adjusted, traffic moves smoothly in both directions. However, if conditions change and traffic gets heavier in one direction, the amount of green light time in that direction should be increased. If the traffic lights are not adjusted, the traffic will back up, resulting in many unhappy users of that intersection.

Controls must be continually monitored to determine when adjustments are needed. The police continually monitor traffic lights to be assured they are properly adjusted. When they notice traffic backed up in one direction, they notify the traffic control department and the necessary adjustments are made. It is through monitoring, analysis, and adjustment that controls continue to meet the needs of users. Computer systems require the monitoring, analysis, and adjustment of controls.

CONTROL DEVELOPMENT LIFE CYCLE (CDLC)

After controls are designed, three steps remain in the CDLC: to get feedback information on controls, analyze that information, and make any necessary adjustment. The adequate execution of these three steps determines the effectiveness of controls.

The feedback step is necessary to measure the effectiveness of controls. For example, the objective of control in a credit card system is to prevent bad charges from being made. Controls normally include a telephone call by the merchant if the sale is over $50 and looking up card numbers in a listing of credit cards whose credit has been permanently or temporarily suspended. In this sytem feedback mechanisms provide information on the frequency and amount of bad charges. Without this type of information, the credit card company could not tell if its controls were effective.

Equally as important as getting feedback information is analyzing that data. Experience has shown that with computer crimes, the feedback information necessary to detect the defalcation is usually available. Unfortunately, in many organizations the feedback information is not analyzed. Thus computer crimes are allowed to continue when they could be prevented. Analysis is analyzing the information available about controls to determine whether controls are meeting their objective. In other words, it tells how effective the controls are.

Based on this analysis, adjustments may be necessary. This is the step for which feedback information is gathered and analyzed. It would be inexcusable not to make an adjustment once a control weakness has been uncovered.

The CDLC is illustrated in Figure 9.1. Note that this process was covered in Chapter 5 to explain what should be done. It is repeated in this chapter to emphasize the feedback, analysis, and adjustment parts of the control process.

COLLECTING FEEDBACK INFORMATION

Feedback information is needed for all areas of control. It is just as important to get feedback information about operational controls as

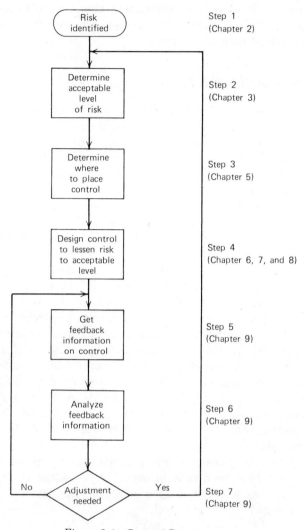

Figure 9.1   **Control** Process.

it is for application and environmental controls. Feedback information should be provided from each and every control. Without feedback information, there is no assurance that a control is operative.

When an individual control is designed, the designer should also specify the type of feedback information needed from that control. For example, let's examine some controls on an "hours worked" field used in a payroll application. One control might be a range check to determine that the hours worked is no less than 20 and no greater than 60. Two types of feedback information might be requested from this check. The first is an error message requesting action when the hours worked field is outside the specified range (i.e., less than 20 or greater than 60). The second type of feedback information might list the number of times that error message was produced and/or the department whose employee's hours fell outside the specified limit.

The types of monitoring desired by management specify the feedback information required. For example, if error trend information will not be used for analysis purposes, there is no reason to provide that type of feedback data for that purpose. However, certain types of adjustments can be made when trend feedback information is available.

Many systems analysts, when they design controls, do not spend sufficient time specifying feedback information. This aspect of controls can be complex. First, the analyst must determine what control is needed, which must anticipate what might go wrong with the normal processing. This is further complicated by the fact that feedback information must anticipate what can go wrong with the controls designed to monitor what might go wrong with normal processing. It is a difficult task to accomplish.

Feedback information is collected from a variety of sources. Ideally, automated controls provide most of the feedback information, but this is not always true. Many times, feedback from manual sources proves valuable in assessing automated controls. For example, customer complaints frequently pinpoint some serious problems in automated controls or problems that are difficult for automated controls to detect.

There are two types of feedback information. The first, direct feedback information, is information created solely for the purpose of feedback analysis. The second type of feedback information is indirect, which is information available from independent sources and can be used for feedback purposes but is not specifically prepared for feedback analysis (see Exhibit 9.1 for sources of feedback information).

Direct Feedback Information

Direct feedback normally monitors compliance to a specific control. The feedback information provides the operating characteristics of a control, such as the number of times it was executed, the result of that execution, and characteristics about the execution. For example, feedback information on a security guard might indicate which

Exhibit 9.1   Sources of Feedback Information

Direct Feedback

  Error messages

  Suspense files

  Normal reports

  Trend analysis files

  Control reports

  Hardware indicators

  Extracts from data files

Indirect Feedback

  Users

  Customers

  Management

  Auditors (internal and external)

  Quality assurance groups

  User groups

  Fact finding and interviews

  Software logs

  Government reports

---

individuals entered an area, what time they entered and left, and who authorized them to enter, as well as who attempted access but was denied access because proper authorization was not granted.

Feedback information can be positive or negative. Positive feedback information provides an indication that events have occurred. For example, if every individual entering an area were required to sign a log, the log would be a positive feedback on the control, which is the security guard. Negative feedback information provides information only on control violations. For example, if a security guard checked employee badges, there would be no feedback information on people who had a security pass. The negative feedback information would be given only on those individuals who did not have a security badge and thus were required to sign a log to gain entry into an area, or were denied access.

Whether feedback is positive or negative is dependent on the situation being controlled. Negative information is more common in automated systems. However, in some cases positive feedback on each transaction processed is desirable. In computer terminal operations, for example, when a person enters a code, the system can give positive feedback showing the meaning of that code so that the individual entering information can be assured processing will be correct.

Direct feedback information normally requires the systems analyst to design the feedback mechanisms. Some of the more common direct feedback mechanisms are:

- *Error Messages* An indication that a problem has occurred. Error messages normally indicate what type of error occurred, the condition that caused the error, and information sufficient to identify the error, if practical.

- *Suspense Files* A repository of feedback information about problems in a system. For example, in a cash payments system, a suspense file might be established for unidentified payments.

- *Normal Reports* The normal outputs of a system containing information that serves a dual purpose. First, they are helpful in the operations of the system, and, second, they provide feedback information on controls. For example, normal reports may indicate the number of batches included in the report. This is valuable both for feedback to ensure data is complete and to give the users of the report an appreciation of the volume of transactions included in the report.

- *Trend Analysis File* A special report of feedback information that indicates the severity and direction of problems over an extended period of time. For example, trend analysis might be done on keypunching errors. This would indicate if the keypunch operators are getting better, worse, or staying the same in respect to the number of errors made.

- *Control Reports* Special reports prepared for the purpose of providing feedback information on controls. These may be continuous reports (e.g., issued every day, week, or month) or may be issued when unusual conditions occur. A control report on budgets might show the budget year-to-date and actual expenditures year-to-date. This control report provides people feedback information on their spending. However, if actual expenditures exceeded the budgeted amount by 20% or more, a special control report might be issued showing all the departments and/or accounts in that overrun status.

- *Hardware Indicators* Hardware devices with dials, lights, and alarms to signal control violations. For example, a fire alarm will sound if a fire occurs, dials may go into danger zones if temperature controls are violated, and flashing lights or bells can indicate a vehicle is approaching and you should be cautious.
- *Extracts from Data Files* Specific extracts of information available in computer files and extracted for the purpose of being presented as control information. These special-purpose extracts are normally done with a query or report writing language.

Indirect Feedback Information

Many sources provide information on the functioning of control. Indirect information is normally obtained from a third party.

Many parties have a vested interest in the correct functioning of a computerized business application. Some of these concerns are related to their job function, whereas others are related to the work they are being required to perform. For example, auditors are interested in the controls of computer systems because part of their function is to assess the adequacy of control. On the other hand, customers of a system want their own records processed correctly and thus provide feedback when that processing does not occur properly.

Third-party information can be both positive and negative. Positive information is given when the third party lets you know that something is right or wrong. Negative feedback assumes that if you do not hear from the users and customers of the system, everything is okay. However, third-party negative information could represent an "I don't care" attitude.

If payroll checks are sent out to all employees of an organization, one could assume that if employees do not complain, they are not underpaid. Perhaps a few wealthy employees do not take the time to verify the correctness of their check, but most employees do. Therefore, in a system such as payroll, there is probably a very high correlation between adequacy of the system and employee complaints. In another system, such as order entry, customers whose orders are ignored may choose not to complain but, rather, to go to another organization to have their needs satisfied. Therefore, the lack of customer complaints may not indicate that an order entry system is functioning correctly. There are other types of feedback information that are helpful. By monitoring orders of the better customers, a dropoff in orders may indicate customer dissatisfaction.

Indirect feedback information requires no specific act by the systems analyst to gather that information. However, the systems analyst may need to do some investigating to determine whether the desired type of indirect feedback information is available. Once the indirect feedback information is known to be in existence, it can be gathered and used for control analysis purposes.

The more common types of indirect feedback information are:

- *Users* Users of a system are an excellent source of feedback information. For example, the people in the payroll department can tell you many of the good and bad points about a computerized payroll application.

- *Customers* Third party individuals who work with a system quickly come to recognize its advantages and limitations. They are the people who really know the effectiveness and efficiency of a computerized application.

- *Management* Management has the primary responsibility for control. Therefore, management should be overseeing and evaluating the adequacy of the control system. The results of its investigation should provide valuable feedback to analysts, which can be used to adjust controls to better meet the needs of the organization.

- *Auditors (Internal and External)* One of the functions most organizations assign to their internal auditors is assessing the adequacy of the system of internal control. In conducting this assessment, auditors prepare extensive supporting documentation of weaknesses and normally prepare reports outlining those weaknesses. External auditors provide the same type of function, but tend to concentrate on financial controls.

- *Quality Assurance Groups* Many data processing departments have established a quality assurance group within their departments. The objective of these groups is to ensure that the goals, methods, and performance of computerized applications meet the design specifications, standards, and needs of the organization.

- *User Groups* Many industries have specialized user groups for their industry, such as banking, petroleum, and the drug industry. In addition, other user groups are established to help utilize specific pieces of computer hardward and/or other system aids. These groups provide systems personnel an opportunity to interact with their peers, and thus provide insight into how other organizations are addressing control. This may prove helpful in evaluating the performance of controls in existing and planned systems.

- *Fact Finding and Interviews*   There is no better way to find out something than to ask. Many organizations regularly investigate the adequacy of control through questioning, and they send questionnaires to users. The results are categorized according to problem areas of internal control.

- *Software Logs*   Many of the larger software packages have associated with them a log listing usage and control violations. For example, the IBM Corporation offers Systems Management Facility (SMF), which maintains a record of every job start, job stop, file open and close, attempted security violations, as well as job accounting information. The SMF log contains a large amount of control information, even though it was primarily established as a vehicle for charging users for the use of data processing resources.

- *Government Reports*   Many governmental organizations issue information about specific industries and problems. For example, the U.S. General Accounting Office regularly issues audit reports about problems associated with computers. Although these relate to specific government agencies, many of the lessons also would be appropriate and helpful in controlling systems in private industry.

FEEDBACK INFORMATION ANALYSIS

An essential step to ensuring the continual adequacy of control in computerized systems is feedback information analysis. It is only through this analysis that organizations can detect control problems, and, until detected, these problems cannot be corrected.

Control analysis is a continuing function. Depending on the system characteristics, this analysis function may be performed continuously, daily, weekly, or monthly. What is important is that the analysis function be performed on a regular basis.

Feedback analysis is a responsibility of both the user of the application and the data processing department. For example, the payroll department should analyze payroll feedback information, while the data processing department should be analyzing those aspects of payroll feedback information that relate to the operation of the system, such as file response time and errors as an indicator of systems problems.

A study of computer fraud indicates that the feedback information necessary to detect those frauds was available. Unfortunately, that feedback information was not analyzed, and thus the fraud was not detected. Much of this failure is due to misuse of feedback information.

One of the main reasons feedback information is not used is that it is not presented in the proper format. If it is difficult to obtain feedback information, to find what is needed within the feedback information provided, or to understand what the data means, people will not go to the effort of using it to analyze problems.

Part of the problem in understanding feedback information is that the feedback information is not in the proper format for easy use. For example, error listings indicate what type of errors occur. To determine the frequency of a particular error would require sitting down with many listings and manually accumulating the errors according to type. The difficulty and time involved in doing this may hamper an individual's interest in putting feedback information in a usable format and dampen the desire to do so.

There are numerous feedback analysis tools available to the systems analyst for this purpose. The analyst should approach feedback analysis as he or she would any other aspect of systems design. The analyst has others' needs to satisfy and must provide control-oriented people with sufficient tools so that they can effectively analyze the available feedback information. In the performance of this function, the analyst should do the following:

- Determine the specific needs of the control-oriented people.
- Determine whether the information necessary to satisfy those needs is available.
- If the information is not available, determine whether it can be economically obtained.
- Design feedback reports that will be useful to control-oriented people.
- Design systems that will produce those reports.
- Document how those reports are used.
- Obtain concurrence from the users of feedback information that the proposed reports truly satisfy their needs.
- Implement the feedback reports.

There are two aspects to analyzing feedback information. The first is organizing the information for analysis purposes. Controls provide feedback information, but it must be organized so that it can be used. The second aspect is analyzing the information once it has

Exhibit 9.2   Methods of Feedback Analysis

Organizing information for analysis

    Reorganization

    Summarization

    Trend analysis

    Comparison

    Limits

    Stratification

    Algorithms

    Sampling

    Ratios and percentages

    Pictoral presentation

Analysis methods

    Interview analysis

    Judgment

    Testing

    Comparison to standards (i.e., specifications)

    Simulation/modeling

    Automatic transaction initiation

---

been organized and properly presented (see Exhibit 9.2 for a list of the methods for organizing and analyzing feedback information).

Organizing Information for Analysis

Most feedback information is a by-product of normal computer operations. It takes the form of error messages, interim processing results that may indicate a problem or trend, and questionable data. Interim processing results include such things as purchases made at lower than normal prices, but not so low as to be questioned or rejected. Questionable transactions are those normally requiring additional investigation or at least a warning message to alert people to a possible problem, such as an employee being paid for more than 100 hours per week.

Feedback information normally requires some processing to put it in a format that facilitates analysis. Some of the approaches used in this formatting include:

- *Reorganization* Feedback information is sorted into a new sequence. For example, feedback information may be in time sequence, but having it in a location or area affected sequence would be much more meaningful.

- *Summarization* The data by itself is of little value, but by summarizing the data into one or more levels of totals the information becomes meaningful for feedback analysis. For example, if we were to analyze computer errors, individual errors would be of little value, but the number of errors categorized by type or source of entry may be meaningful.

- *Trend Analysis* The direction of an event is shown over a period of time. For example, the number of days between billing and payment is of little value by itself, but a trend showing whether it is getting shorter or longer can indicate when action needs to be taken.

- *Comparison* Frequently, feedback information by itself is meaningless, and only has value when compared to other information. For example, suppose that both branch A and branch B have 10 errors of type X. Until we know the size of the population on which those errors occurred, we may not be able to understand the significance of those figures. For example, if branch A had 5000 transactions and made 10 errors, the situation would not be nearly as serious as that of branch B if it had only 85 transactions and made 10 errors.

- *Limits* Predetermined tolerances can be established for feedback information. Only the feedback information that exceeds those tolerances is reported for analysis purposes. For example, sales personnel may have leeway in establishing the price they charge customers for a particular product. Control feedback may look for prices that vary from the normal price by greater than plus or minus 10%. Thus deviations within the limits of plus or minus 10% are not reported for feedback analysis purposes, but those transactions exceeding those limits are reported.

- *Stratification* Feedback information is placed into classifications of data by dollar amount. For example, if purchase orders are analyzed to evaluate the efficiency of purchasing, the orders may be classified or stratified into amounts of $10 and less, $10 to

$25, $25 to $50, $50 to $100, and more than $100. If it costs the organization $5 to process a purchase order, it would be important to know how many purchase orders are less than the cost of processing the order itself, and so on.

- *Algorithms* Information for analysis may be selected based on satisfying a series of criteria, or, in other words, a selection algorithm. For example, in analyzing collection controls, feedback information might structure that data to show customers whose payments were more than 45 days old, whose balance exceeded $250, who ordered less than $1000 of the product in the past 12 months, and so on.

- *Sampling* Feedback on the accuracy of processing may be evaluated based on a sample of that processing for further analysis. This is similar to quality control in a factory, in which the quality of the products is verified using randomly selected products. If an organization wants to know that its invoices are correct, it may select every hundredth invoice, starting with a different number each day. The unique number would be the last number of the invoice so that the sample would be random.

- *Ratios and Percentages*   Percentage shows what part of the whole a particular item comprises. For example, error X comprises 10% of all errors. Ratios show the relationship between two variables; for example, the ratio of error X to error Y may be $3:2$, or three errors of type X are made to every two errors of type Y.

- *Pictorial Presentation* Feedback information is shown by a graph, chart, or other pictorial presentation. For example, when analyzing errors by individual operator, a bar chart provides data in a pictorial format that is easy to analyze.

ANALYSIS METHODS

The proper presentation of feedback information performs much of the analysis. For example, in our analysis of the efficiency of purchase orders, we could quickly assess the cost-effectiveness of the purchasing process by the number of low-value purchase orders. If a large number of purchase orders were less than $10, we could speculate that purchasing inefficiency was the cause.

The feedback information is organized for analysis purposes, and then it is analyzed. This analysis is normally performed by people, although some organizations automate the analysis process. A common example of automated analysis is in the control over adequacy of inventory. When inventory drops below a predetermined amount, the feedback information is automatically analyzed and a purchase order is issued.

The techniques used to analyze feedback information are:

- *Interview Analysis* Based on the information provided in the feedback report, people substantiate the seriousness of the condition by interviewing other people; in other words, they ask other people to help with the analysis. The results of these interviews may result in action being taken, dependent, of course, on the guidance given in the interviews.
- *Judgment* A member in a position of authority makes a decision about what action needs to be taken based on the feedback information. That individual uses his or her experience and skills to determine whether action should be taken, and, if action should be taken, what type.
- *Testing* The analysis of feedback information may raise questions or leave doubts in the mind of the individual performing the analysis. In such a case, that individual determines that the validity of the feedback information must be substantiated through testing because he or she is uncertain whether:
  - The feedback information is representative of the entire population. For example, the results of a sample of processing could be a sampling error.
  - The feedback information represents an unusual occurrence rather than a trend condition. For example, a high-frequency error in one week may indicate that the full-time employees are on vacation and temporary help may be causing temporary problems.
  - An error occurred in the feedback collection.
  - An error occurred in the organization of the feedback information and/or in the presentation of the information.
- *Comparison to Standards (i.e., Specifications)* The person analyzing the feedback information uses the systems specification standards as a basis for analyzing the meaning of the feedback information. For example, if an on-line system has been designed to provide a three-second response time, then, when analyzing response time feedback information, that three-second standard would be the basis of determining systems performance.

- *Simulation/Modeling* Feedback information can be fed into a model to project or simulate what the actual processing should have been. For example, some banks feed selected feedback information into a banking model in an effort to verify the cash position of each branch at the end of the day. If the actual cash position of a branch varies significantly from the simulated amounts, this causes additional investigation to be undertaken. In other instances, processing characteristics are fed into a model in an effort to anticipate processing problems. This type of modeling can predict such things as when a data base should be reorganized.

- *Automatic Transaction Initiation* The most sophisticated method of feedback analysis is automated analysis. This utilizes the power of the computer to take action or make adjustments based on the analysis of feedback information. A previous example illustrated automatic inventory replenishment. Other examples of automatic transaction initiation are accounts receivable dunning notices, automatic requests to customers to reorder products such as magazine subscriptions, and default options that substitute a standard value for one that does not appear reasonable or is left out.

These are not meant to form an exhaustive list of the methods for organizing and analyzing feedback information; rather, the list describes the more commonly used methods. Systems designers should select those methods that best meet the objectives of feedback analysis for their systems. The analysis of this feedback analysis may result in changes to the computerized business application. These changes should be documented, and the changes themselves categorized and analyzed to determine the performance of the computerized business application.

CHANGES TO COMPUTERIZED BUSINESS APPLICATIONS

The performance of a system can be measured by the amount of maintenance effort allocated to that system. This effort can be indicative of poor systems design, extensive changes in systems specifications by the user, or a combination of the two. However, it is important for data processing management to analyze this systems change information in an effort to evaluate systems performance.

By examining systems change records, management can determine when systems should be replaced. This same concept is used in many production areas. For example, a film manufacturing organization can determine the wearout rate of cameras by analyzing the number of good pictures per roll. A drop in the number of good pictures per roll indicates that cameras are wearing out. Likewise, an increase in the number of changes and/or the cost of changes can be indicative that the computer system is wearing out.

In performing this maintenance analysis, organizations should categorize the type of maintenance that occurs. Categories valuable for this purpose are:

- *Critical Maintenance (Immediate)* Maintenance that is required before a system can be run. For example, if a system "hangs up," the problem must be fixed before the system can be restrated.

- *Critical Maintenance (More Than Two Days)* Changes of the highest priority to a system but not of the type that needs to be fixed on the spot. For example, a pricing error uncovered due to a programming problem has a high priority for correction, but the system could still be run and clerks could manually pull all the erroneous invoices for manual correction at a later time.

- *Normal Maintenance (One-Time Change)* The routine systems changes for situations that will occur only a few times. This would include special extracts, special reports, and changes of a limited time duration, such as a special sales promotion.

- *Normal Maintenance (Within Three Months)* The normal changes to a computerized system with an installation date of less than three months from the time the systems analyst is notified of the change.

- *Normal Maintenance (More Than Three Months)* Systems changes for which the systems analyst has more than three months' notice. These are normally either large changes or changes of a very low priority.

One allocation of maintenance effort among the various types is illustrated in Exhibit 9.3, which is based on a study made by a large data processing organization. The amount of effort is calculated based on hours of systems analyst/programmer time expended for each type of maintenance.

Analysis of this type made by an organization would show different maintenance patterns for different systems. By analyzing these

Exhibit 9.3   Allocation of Maintenance Effort

Type of Maintenance	Effort %
Critical maintenance—immediate	1
Critical maintenance—more than two days	17
Normal maintenance—one-time change	27
Normal maintenance—within three months	19
Normal maintenance—more than three months	36
Total	100

charts, management can quickly distinguish those systems that have developed a pattern of a continual need for critical maintenance from those systems that have an orderly, structured maintenance pattern. This analysis provides some insight into the amount of control direction provided by the user of the system. Those operating a system on a continual crash basis (i.e., in need of a continual critical maintenance) normally have systems indicative of other control problems. This analysis of maintenance is a good indicator of control problems in a computerized business system.

Program maintenance should be regularly monitored by documenting all the changes to computerized applications. Ideally, these maintenance changes should be prenumbered and approved. A program/module maintenance control form is illustrated in Figure 9.2. The purpose of this form is to show a history of maintenance for each individual program or system module.

The form shows the organization, system, and user representative for that particular program. The user representative is the individual responsible for approving changes to that module. The form has a section to describe the program, its size, date completed, the programming language, who specified the program, and who did the programming. The history segment of the form shows each change request number, who made the change, and when. If the change was not made, the word "voided" is put in the "changed by" column.

SUMMARY

The CDLC is a procedure to help ensure the effectiveness of controls. This process recognizes that controls must be continually adjusted to

Program/Module Maintenance Control Form

Page   of ____

Project no.

Oganization _____

Program number _____

Programmer _____

System _____

User representative _____

Programming description

Description of program/module:

_____

_____

_____

_____

Programmin size _____ Data completed _____ Language _____

Specifications done by _____   Date _____   Programming done by _____   Date

Maintenance history

No.	Change/ request no.	Changed by	Date	No.	Change/ request no.	Changed by	Date
1.				7.			
2.				8.			
3.				9.			
4.				10.			
5.				11.			
6.				12.			

Figure 9.2 **Program/Module Maintenance Control Form.**

remain effective. The control process begins by designing controls to reduce risks to an acceptable level. Once the risk has been identified and an acceptable level of loss agreed on, the control should be designed and monitored. When the control fails to achieve the acceptable level of loss, it should be adjusted to bring the loss into the acceptable range. Using these concepts, control design is moved from an art to a science.

Index